Instructions
YOU ARE DIFFERENT

No two people in the world are alike. Not all Virgos are methodical; not all Leos are lordly; not all Scorpios are highly sexed. Everyone is different, and you must know more than the birth sign (Sun Sign) in order to understand yourself and others through Astrology.

Dial-A-Scope quickly and accurately shows the HOW and WHY of individual differences, and makes Astrology more understandable and useful.

HOW TO USE DIAL-A-SCOPE

To learn INDIVIDUALITY, set the SUN SIGN:

1. Rotate the large wheel so that signs on wheel match signs on the outermost (stationary) circle.
2. Holding the large wheel so that it will not move, turn SUN Indicator (☉) to the **center** of the correct Sun Sign, matching the birth date to the date periods in the large stationary circle. This will show the placement of the sun in the horoscope.
3. To learn INDIVIDUALITY, turn to the pages in the section that follows page 5 and read the information found under the proper Sun Sign.

To learn PERSONALITY, set the ASCENDANT:

1. On the outermost rim of the stationary circle are the Hours of Birth (with 12 NOON at the top, and 12 MIDNIGHT at bottom). Holding **both** the large plastic wheel and the SUN Indicator **together**, rotate **both** until the SUN Indicator (☉) points to the closest Hour of Birth. (See page 2 for detailed Hour of Birth information.)
2. After having set the Hour of Birth note which sign (Leo, Taurus, Virgo, etc.) on the **large plastic wheel** is between 4 A.M. and 6 A.M. This sign is the Sign Ascending—the ASCENDANT.
3. Read the PERSONALITY (Ascendant) in the section following page 19.

To learn MENTALITY, set the MOON SIGN:

1. See page 36 for simple instructions for determining Moon Sign.
2. After you have read how to determine the proper Moon Sign, move the MOON Indicator (☾) to the center of the correct Moon Sign wherever that sign is located on the **large plastic wheel**.
3. Turn to page 27 and learn the MENTALITY by reading the section that follows page 27.

Learn more from the SUN'S HOUSE NUMBER:

1. Note that the large stationary circle has House Numbers—*i.e.,* 1st House, 2nd House, etc.
2. Note in which house the SUN Indicator (☉) is located, and read the section starting with page 31 to find the meaning of the Sun in House Number.

Learn more from the MOON'S HOUSE NUMBER:

1. Find the correct House Number where the MOON Indicator (☾) is positioned.
2. Note in which house the MOON Indicator lies and read the section starting on page 33.

Copyright © Arco Publishing Company, Inc., 1970

Consider ASPECTS (If Any)

See page 35. (Aspects — favorable and unfavorable — can modify or change individual characteristics, and provide reasons for even more individual differences.)

Learn MORE by further DELINEATION

If desired, further reading of the native's Chart may be done with Astrology Dial-A-Scope. For this additional information and further understanding, follow the suggestions below.
1. Skip any House already occupied by the Sun or Moon.
2. Begin with 1st House if it is not occupied by Sun or Moon.
3. Note the "affairs" or matters ruled by the House being studied. (These affairs are written on the inner circle in each House division.)
4. Note the Sign ON PLASTIC WHEEL which is positioned in (rules) the House being studied.
5. Turn to Sun Signs (pages 5—17). Read the description given for that Sign (as determined in 4 above). Learn the native's inner feelings (Individuality) about the affairs of that House.
6. Turn to Ascendants (pages 19—26). Read the description given for the same Sign (as above). Gain insight as to how the individual's Personality acts and reacts to the affairs of that House.
7. Turn to Moon Signs (pages 27—30). Read the description given for that same Sign. Get a better understanding of how the Mentality works for or against the individual's affairs of that House.
8. Repeat the same process with all Houses not occupied by Sun or Moon. (Note: Aspects should also be considered.)

HOUR OF BIRTH

Example: For a 5:30 A.M. birth hour, set Sun Indicator, along with plastic wheel, **midway** between the 4 A.M. — 6 A.M. section. **Always** set Sun Indicator half-way between the proper 2 hour division. Such a setting gives the proper Ascendant, and an accurate reading.

Note: If birth time is thought to be exactly on a dividing hour (2 A.M., 8 P.M., etc.), it will be necessary to try 2 settings of the Sun Indicator and plastic wheel together.

Example: For a 6 A.M. birth hour, first set Sun Indicator (in center of proper Sun Sign on plastic wheel) in 4 A.M. — 6 A.M. section, and read the appropriate descriptions as indicated by this setting. (See Ascendant instructions on page 1.) If the readings do not fit the native at all, the actual birth time likely was **after** 6 A.M. In which case, re-set wheel and Sun Indicator between 6 A.M. — 8 A.M. section, and read correct descriptions.

Special Note: If birth hour is not known, try to narrow time down to day/night, morning/afternoon, etc. Then try different settings and their separate readings as described on page 1 and above until correct hour is determined.

OR, a SOLAR Chart may be set. The Solar Chart places the Sun Sign as the Ascendant, and in the 1st House. This Chart will not be as complete as the known-birth-time chart, but will describe Sun Sign characteristics, and show Aspects accurately.

Contents

Dial-A-Scope
Instructions .... 1 & 2

THE SUN – YOUR INDIVIDUALITY 5
Sun in Aries 6
Sun in Taurus 7
Sun in Gemini 8
Sun in Cancer 9
Sun in Leo 10
Sun in Virgo 11
Sun in Libra 12
Sun in Scorpio 13
Sun in Sagittarius 14
Sun in Capricorn 15
Sun in Aquarius 16
Sun in Pisces 17

THE ASCENDANT – YOUR PERSONALITY 19
Aries Ascending 20
Taurus Ascending 20
Gemini Ascending 21
Cancer Ascending 21
Leo Ascending 22
Virgo Ascending 23
Libra Ascending 23
Scorpio Ascending 24
Sagittarius Ascending 24
Capricorn Ascending 25
Aquarius Ascending 26
Pisces Ascending 26

THE MOON – YOUR MENTALITY 27
Moon in Aries 28
Moon in Taurus 28
Moon in Gemini 28
Moon in Cancer 28
Moon in Leo 29
Moon in Virgo 29
Moon in Libra 29
Moon in Scorpio 29
Moon in Sagittarius 30
Moon in Capricorn 30
Moon in Aquarius 30
Moon in Pisces 30

SUN IN HOUSES (1 – 6) 31
SUN IN HOUSES (7 – 12) 32
MOON IN HOUSES (1 – 6) 33
MOON IN HOUSES (7 – 12) 34
THE ASPECTS 35

Elbert Wade's MOON TABLES (1900–1980) 36
Astro-Tips 78

ELBERT WADE, well-known Astrologer, educator, and writer invented and designed ASTROLOGY DIAL-A-SCOPE after years of study and personal research so that YOU can benefit from a better understanding of yourself and others using man's oldest science and art — Astrology. DIAL-A-SCOPE lets you know Astrology's truths INSTANTLY . . . without wasting time and money on stacks of books which are often too complicated or too general to give any actually individualized information.

The Sun -- Your Individuality

Without the Sun, there would be no life. It is the principal driving force behind the whole solar system. In your Horoscope, it represents will-power, vitality, strength, leadership, creativity, the urge to achieve, high office, positions of title and rank, new undertakings, publicity, popularity — in essence, your inner nature, your Individuality. It symbolizes how you really are inside, how you really feel and sense, and react. The Sun and its placement in your Horoscope is the most important single factor in the entire Chart. Your Sun Sign is determined by your date of birth in the Solar month, not the calendar month. Each individual is one Sign or another. Persons born within three days before and three days after the change of Solar months are said to be born in the "Cusp" which causes them to be more complex — taking on characteristics of the two Sun Signs.

Sun in Aries

Aries ♈ *The Ram (March 21 — April 19)*
Ruler: Mars (♂); Birthstone: Diamond
Lucky Day: Tuesday; Key Words: "I am."

Aries is a Fire Sign and masculine. It governs the head and face. The Sun in Aries gives the native much mental energy and a quick wit. Ariens are pioneers and natural leaders, normally full of impulsive ambition, enterprise, and new ideas. The desire is to lead, not to follow. Often they are fiery and quick tempered, continually ready to resent abuse or imposition to themselves or others. They are not inclined to hold grudges for long. Ariens, because of their love of justive and freedom for all, coupled with their drive and self-will, can too easily go to extremes with their sharp tongues, or lack of discretion. They are persistent to a point, but may give up too soon if things don't happen quickly enough to suit them. They are not, however, easily discouraged. They often rush in where angels fear to tread.

Arien Careers: Policeman, fireman, military commander, prizefighter, surgeon, butcher, metal worker, barber, hairdresser, hat designer or manufacturer, teacher, lecturer, salesman, dentist, carpenter, engineer, mechanic, cutler, optometrist.

Sex, Love, Marriage: Most Suitable: Leo, Sagittarius. **Suitable:** Gemini, Libra, Aquarius. **Possible:** Cancer, Scorpio, Pisces, Aries. **Least Suitable:** Capricorn, Taurus, Virgo.

Famous Sun in Aries Persons: Doris Day, Gregory Peck, Charlie Chaplin, Warren Beatty, Virgil Grisson, General Booth, Tennessee Williams, Bette Davis, Bismarck, John P. Morgan, Sr.

Sun in Taurus

TAURUS ♉ The Bull *(April 20 – May 20)*
Ruler: Venus (♀); Birthstone: Emerald
Lucky Day: Friday; Key Words: "I have."

Taurus is an Earth Sign and feminine. It governs the throat and neck. A Taurus Sun inclines the native to be self-reliant, determined, persistent, stable, firm, stubborn, careful, and concerned with outcomes. Taureans are especially sensitive to pain — emotional as well as physical. Normally they possess unbelievable patience. They can wait a very long time for their "ship" to come in. By nature they are as gentle as a cow, but can be as reckless as a bull in a china shop when pushed to real anger. Taurus can be stubborn to the point of being unyielding, and can be quite secretive, but is normally highly practical and constructive. Often the main interests are materialistic in nature. They like money, comfort, security, and all the "good" things of life.

<u>Taurean Careers</u>: Banker, cashier, credit manager, treasurer, stock broker, throat specialist, commercial artist, interior decorator, gardener, farmer, jewelry designer, musician, singer, public speaker, florist, social worker, throat-wear designer.

<u>Sex, Love, Marriage</u>: **Most Suitable:** Virgo, Capricorn. **Suitable:** Cancer, Scorpio, Pisces. **Possible:** Libra, Aquarius, Gemini, Taurus. **Least Suitable:** Aries, Leo, Sagittarius.

<u>Famous Sun in Taurus Persons</u>: William Shakespeare, Henry Ford, Shirley MacLaine, Sandra Dee, Harry Truman, Bing Crosby, Willie Mays, Perry Como, Kate Smith, Liberace.

Sun in Gemini

GEMINI ♊ **The Twins** *(May 21 – June 20)*
Ruler: Mercury (☿); Birthstone: Agate
Lucky Day: Wednesday; Key Words: "I think."

Gemini is an Air Sign and masculine. It governs the hands, arms, lungs, and the nervous system. Geminians are basically changeable by nature. Most natives are sympathetic, kind-hearted, and affectionate. They possess a very active and restless mind that is in constant need of new and different avenues of experience. Gemini is an experimenter, an investigator, a quick reasoner, a researcher — talents which can lead to writing. Gemini must be busy, and may work at two or more jobs or hobbies at the same time. They do, however, prefer to work their own way. Gemini is variable, inquiring, and doubtful by nature. Often they marry more than once, or in some way lead a double life. Good conversationalists, they often possess a charming and ready sense of humor.

<u>Geminian Careers:</u> Sales, newspaper reporter, teacher, radio or television announcer, public relations, secretary, typist, stenographer, court reporter, telephone operator, receptionist, writer, pilot, bus driver, postal employee, horologist, comic, mimic.

<u>Sex, Love, Marriage:</u> **Most Suitable:** Libra, Aquarius. **Suitable:** Aries, Leo, Sagittarius. **Possible:** Virgo, Cancer. **Least Suitable:** Pisces, Scorpio, Taurus, Capricorn, Gemini.

<u>Famous Sun in Gemini Persons:</u> Judy Garland, John F. Kennedy, Dean Martin, Leslie Uggams, Bob Hope, Paul McCartney, Stan Laurel, John Wayne, Queen Victoria, Robert Cummings.

Sun in Cancer

CANCER ♋ **The Crab** *(June 21 – July 22)*
Ruler: Moon (☽); Birthstone: Ruby or Moonstone
Lucky Day: Monday; Key Words: "I feel."

Cancer is a Water Sign and feminine. It governs the breast and stomach. The Sun in Cancer reflects a quiet, reserved, retiring, and highly sensitive individual, but one who loves publicity. Cancerians are usually quite versatile, changeable, and moody. They are subject to frequent "ups and downs" in attitudes, vocations, and love. They are, none-the-less, determined in their goals and opinions. They normally do have fertile imaginations and a dramatic ability to take others ideas and promote them for their own purposes. Cancers' highly receptive nature makes them easily influenced by their environment. Sun in Cancer blesses with a retentive memory. They usually are industrious, prudent, frugal, sympathetic, and highly sensitive to any criticism. There is love for the home, mother, and the past. Often Cancerians accumulate a lot of money.

Cancerian Careers: Hotel-motel management, catering, cook, housekeeper, home economist, dietician, interior decorator, furniture designer or manufacturer, writer, child psychologist, children's nurse, shopkeeper — (gifts, novelties, antiques), dairy operator, brewer, politician.

Sex, Love, Marriage: **Most Suitable**: Scorpio, Pisces. **Suitable**: Capricorn, Taurus, Virgo. **Possible**: Leo, Gemini, Libra. **Least Suitable**: Aquarius, Aries, Sagittarius, Cancer.

Famous Sun in Cancer Persons: Phyllis Diller, Ernest Hemingway, Ringo Star, John Glenn, Nelson Rockefeller, John W. Newbern, John Jacob Astor, Van Cliburn, Paul Anka, Rossini.

Sun in Leo

LEO ♌ **The Lion** *(July 23 – August 22)*
Ruler: Sun (☉); Birthstone: Sardonyx
Lucky Day: Sunday; Key Words: "I will."

Leo is a Fire Sign and masculine. It governs the heart and upper back. A Leo Sun gives the native an active mind, a good nature, generosity, and normally many friends because of these qualities. The Leo Sun is a natural leader, ambitious, independent, determined, persistent, honest, and highly industrious. Leos are quick to anger, but may be just as quickly appeased. Normally there is a "sunny" disposition, and a strong tendency for being frank, candid, outspoken, direct, and to the point in all matters. Leo is forceful and greatly appreciates (and demands) recognition and admiration. They are magnetic personalities who are especially good at "selling" themselves and their ideas to others. They have an unquenchable thirst to "show off."

Leos Careers: Government, theater management, acting, speaking, teaching, stock broker, speculator, jeweler, goldsmith, foreman, department head, management, television acting, model, animal trainer, heart specialist, master of ceremonies, vocalist.

Sex, Love, Marriage: **Most Suitable**: Aries, Sagittarius. **Suitable**: Libra, Aquarius, Gemini. **Possible**: Cancer, Pisces, Leo. **Least Suitable**: Scorpio, Capricorn, Taurus, Virgo.

Famous Sun in Leo Persons: Napoleon, Jimmie Dean, Ben Hogan, Lucille Ball, Fidel Castro, Mae West, Henry Ford, Ralph Bunche, Tennyson, Jason Robards, Jr., George B. Shaw.

Sun in Virgo

VIRGO ♍ **The Virgin** *(August 23 – September 22)*
Ruler: Mercury (☿); Birthstone: Sapphire
Lucky Day: Wednesday; Key Words: "I analyze."

Virgo is an Earth Sign and feminine. It governs the lower digestive tract. The Virgo native is usually modest, thoughtful, serious, contemplative, industrious, and desirous of refining the mind through acquiring knowledge. The Sun here highlights study, reasoning ability, and good use of language. Virgos are usually health conscious and tend to take care of themselves so that they seldom show their true age. Virgo has a very quick temper, but would rather talk things out than fight. There is an inborn desire for cleanliness, order, and system in everything. Virgo is idealistic but practical, frugal yet speculative. Virgos would have others think they are "pure," but this is not always the whole story. Virgo has a good mind, but often lets concern with detail spoil the overall view. Highly critical, they are perfectionists by nature.

<u>Virgos Careers</u>: Editor, writer, teacher, statistician, accountant, bookkeeper, file clerk, typist, billing clerk, secretary, physician, nurse, dietician, maid, supply clerk, social worker, art or literary critic, efficiency expert, musician.

<u>Sex, Love, Marriage</u>: **Most Suitable**: Capricorn, Taurus. **Suitable**: Cancer, Scorpio, Pisces. **Possible**: Libra, Aquarius, Gemini, Virgo. **Least Suitable**: Aries, Leo, Sagittarius.

<u>Famous Sun in Virgo Persons</u>: Lyndon B. Johnson, Henry Ford II, Sophia Loren, Leonard Bernstein, David McCallum, Anne Bancroft, Sid Caesar, Grandma Moses, Peter Sellers, Arthur Godfrey.

Sun in Libra

LIBRA ♎ **The Balance** *(September 23 – October 22)*
Ruler: Venus (♀); Birthstone: Opal
Lucky Day: Friday; Key Words: "I balance."

    Libra is an Air Sign and masculine. It governs the kidneys and lower portion of the back. The Libra native loves beauty, tranquility, justice, peace, and harmony. Libra is basically courteous, pleasant, agreeable, and highly sensitive to the feelings and wishes of others. As a rule Libras are even-tempered, affectionate, and quite sympathetic. The true Libra is a natural go-between and peacemaker. Other words which describe the Libra native are: modest, neat, tasteful (fond of bright colors), kind, amiable, generous, amusement-oriented. They highly dislike any work which might get them "dirty." They like to see order, balance, symmetry in the world, and work as much as they can to bring about such a state of conditions. They may be interested in law, chemistry, and accounting – anything to maintain "balance."

<u>Libran Careers</u>: Attorney, judge, art, literary or music critic, personnel director, mediator, diplomat, mathematician, scientist, beauty shop operator, dressmaker or designer, small business owner, painter, illustrator, musician, interior decorator, military officer, marriage counselor.

<u>Sex, Love, Marriage</u>: **Most Suitable**: Aquarius, Gemini. **Suitable**: Aries, Leo, Sagittarius. **Possible**: Virgo, Taurus, Libra. **Least Suitable**: Capricorn, Cancer, Scropio, Pisces.

<u>Famous Sun in Libra Persons</u>: Dwight D. Eisenhower, William Faulkner, Ed Sullivan, Julie Andrews, John Lennon, Oscar Wilde, Helen Hayes, Johnny Carson, Cervantes, Mickey Mantle.

Sun in Scorpio

SCORPIO ♏ The Scorpion *(October 23 – November 21)*
Ruler: Mars (♂); *Birthstone:* Topaz
Lucky Day: Tuesday; *Key Words:* "I desire."

Scorpio is a Water Sign and feminine. It governs the "secrets"—the sex organs and the general area. Scorpios are intense individuals with strong characteristics and shrewd, quick judgments. The native is critical, suspicious, skeptical, but highly enterprising, tenacious, secretive, and possessed of a strong determination. Scorpios are rather fond of the sensuous and material pleasures of life. They are generally economical and calculating. They look for the "buttered side" of the bread. They are inclined to mind their own in matters of business, but are frequently nosey in others' personal lives. They make excellent detectives and investigators. In speech Scropios are frequently direct and blunt, and may even be sarcastic and forceful. They normally possess the drive and desire to succeed at whatever they set their minds to do.

Scorpion Careers: Detective, investigator, policeman, physician, psychiatrist, archeologist, investment broker, sailor, marine, mechanic, funeral director, embalmer, campaign manager, surgeon, butcher, bartender, lifeguard, oil field employee.

Sex, Love, Marriage: **Most Suitable:** Cancer, Pisces. **Suitable:** Capricorn, Taurus, Virgo. **Possible:** Libra, Aquarius, Scorpio. **Least Suitable:** Gemini, Aries, Leo, Sagittarius.

Famous Sun in Scorpio Persons: Pablo Picasso, Richard Burton, Billy Graham, Rock Hudson, Jonas Salk, Martin Luther, Robert Kennedy, Robert Louis Stevenson, Art Carney, Theodore Roosevelt.

Sun in Sagittarius

SAGITTARIUS ⚹ **The Archer** *(November 22 – December 21)*
Ruler: Jupiter (♃); Birthstone: Turquoise
Lucky Day: Thursday; Key Words: "I see."

    Sagittarius is a Fire Sign and masculine. It governs the thighs and hips. The Sagittarius Sun normally produces a jovial, cheery nature, and a person who is hopeful, generous, and charitable. Sagittarians are self-reliant, frank, honest, ambitious, outspoken, persevering to a point, and basically optimistic. Sagittarius loves expansiveness, whether literally so, or mentally so. They will follow if properly asked, but will not be pushed an inch. There is a strong and independent will. They have the ability to "hit the nail right on the head" with what they say — usually without concern as to how others will regard what they say. Sagittarius is sincere, honorable, earnest, aspiring, energetic (mentally, at least), and is possessed of good foresight. Sagittarians frequently are quite "lucky."

<u>Sagittarian Careers</u>: Lawyer, clergyman, editor, publisher, writer, importer, travel agent, foreign correspondent or representative, teacher, philosopher, instructor, vocational guidance counselor, financial advisor, salesman, statesman, advertising executive.

<u>Sex, Love, Marriage</u>: **Most Suitable:** Aries, Leo. **Suitable:** Libra, Aquarius, Gemini. **Possible:** Cancer, Scorpio, Pisces, Sagittarius. **Least Suitable:** Capricorn, Taurus, Virgo.

<u>Famous Sun in Sagittarius Persons</u>: Frank Sinatra, Mary Martin, James Thurber, Walt Disney, Connie Francis, J. Paul Getty, Patty Duke, Winston Churchill, Mark Twain, Spinoza.

Sun in Capricorn

CAPRICORN ♑ The Seagoat *(December 22 – January 19)*
Ruler: Saturn (♄); Birthstone: Garnet
Lucky Day: Saturday; Key Words: "I use."

Capricorn is an Earth Sign and feminine. It governs the knees. Capricornians are by nature quiet, thoughtful, serious, deep-minded, practical, economical, and possessed of good reasoning ability. They act with great dignity and hold a rather high self-esteem. They are particular in all that they do as they aspire to climb higher on the ladder of self-advancement. They are possessed of possibly the greatest perseverance of any other Sign. Capricornians seldom give up on anything they want, even though they are frequently disappointed. Capricorn could be called the "opportunist." They never fail to use whatever or whoever is at hand. Because of their "never say die" natures, it is not uncommon for them to eventually achieve their goals. They are inclined to experience deep depression at times.

Capricornian Careers: Businessman, real estate agent, miner, farmer, building contractor, politician, actor, teacher, social worker, organizer, gardener, veterinarian, executive manager, charity worker, economist, promoter, director.

Sex, Love, Marriage: Most Suitable: Taurus, Virgo. **Suitable:** Cancer, Scorpio, Pisces. **Possible:** Libra, Aquarius, Gemini, Capricorn. **Least Suitable:** Aries, Leo, Sagittarius.

Famous Sun in Capricorn Persons: Richard Nixon, Cary Grant, Elvis Presley, Joan of Arc, Edgar Allan Poe, Louis Pasteur, John Terracina, J.D. Salinger, Sandy Koufax, Danny Kaye.

Sun in Aquarius

AQUARIUS ♒ **The Water Bearer** *(January 20 – February 18)*
Ruler: Uranus (♅); Birthstone: Amethyst
Lucky Day: Saturday; Key Words: "I know."

Aquarius is an Air Sign and masculine. It governs the calves and ankles of the legs. The Sun in Aquarius often develops the native who is basically quiet, patient, reserved, determined, and eccentric in some way or ways. Often this native has ideas which are very advanced and far ahead of the times. Aquarians are usually good reasoners, understanding, tolerant, friendly, generous, charitable, and humanitarian. There is a marked fondness for the occult and "far out" subjects and ideas. While a good friend, Aquarius is more concerned with the benefit of mankind in general than with any individual's problems. They are especially susceptible to acts of kindness, and adore attention and admiration. They might even head up their own self-admiration society, if necessary. There is an interest in broad concepts as opposed to everyday detail.

Aquarian Careers: Social worker, mediator, politician, professor, inventor, scientist, electrician, radio-television repairman, airplane mechanic, motion picture producer, telephone operator, lighting specialist, telegrapher, Astrologer, writer.

Sex, Love, Marriage: Most Suitable: Libra, Gemini. **Suitable:** Aries, Leo, Sagittarius. **Possible:** Aquarius. **Least Suitable:** Cancer, Scorpio, Pisces, Capricorn, Taurus, Virgo.

Famous Sun in Aquarius Persons: Abraham Lincoln, John L. Lewis, Adlai Stevenson, Lord Byron, Douglas MacArthur, Thomas Edison, A. LeRoi Simmons, Dean Rusk, Clark Gable, Jimmy Durante.

Sun in Pisces

PISCES ♓ **The Fishes** *(February 19 – March 20)*
Ruler: Neptune (♆), Birthstone: Aquamarine
Lucky Day: Thursday; Key Words: "I believe."

Pisces is a Water Sign and feminine. It governs the feet. The Pisces native generally has a kind and loving nature. They basically trust everybody until they are disappointed in so doing. Pisceans are inclined to wear their feelings on their sleeves. They are honest, amiable, overly sympathetic, and kind to anything in distress. They are usually neat and particular, and desire order and completeness. One of their problems lies in the inability to make decisions readily. Pisceans frequently tend to timidity and may be lacking in self-confidence. As a rule they are industrious, methodical, and rather logical in their conclusions. Being overly idealistic, imaginative, and inspirational often leads Pisces to emotional scars which might not affect others. There may be a tendency toward periods of extreme moodiness.

<u>Piscean Careers:</u> Psychiatrist, social worker, nurse, private investigator, photographer, creative artist, music, dancing, painting, commercial artist, actor, oil executive or oil field worker, fisherman, sailor, pharmacist, occultist, executive, publisher.

<u>Sex, Love, Marriage:</u> **Most Suitable**: Cancer, Scorpio. **Suitable**: Capricorn, Taurus, Virgo. **Possible**: Pisces. **Least Suitable**: Libra, Aquarius, Gemini, Aries, Leo, Sagittarius.

<u>Famous Sun in Pisces Persons</u>: John Steinbeck, Jackie Gleason, Elizabeth Taylor, George Washington, Victor Hugo, Earl Warren, Luther Burbank, Albert Einstein, Lawrence Welk, Edgar Cayce.

The Ascendant -- Your Personality

Your Ascendant is determined by the hour and place of your birth. The Ascendant ("Rising Sign") is that Sign which is exactly at sunrise point from where you were born, or where you are. Because of the Earth's rotation on its axis, a new Sign of the Zodiac appears on the horizon every 2 hours (and remains in effect for 2 hours), so that in a 24 hour period, all 12 Signs will have passed over that horizon point. Knowing your Ascendant is very important since it determines the House placement for the Sun and other planets. The Sign ascending determines (or modifies) your personal appearance, and how you present your Individuality (your Sun) to the world. Your Ascendant is what others see — it is your Personality.

Aries Ascending

Since Aries rules the head, it is natural that Aries Ascending will have a strong desire to "head-up" whatever is dealt with. Mars, the ruling planet of Aries, gives the individual drive, ambition, aggressiveness, and impulsiveness. Aries Ascending should guard against lack of follow-through. They are very individualistic and impatient, and may have too many irons in the fire to look after all properly. The Fire Sign makes them rather quick tempered. They may blush easily, or turn red in the face when angered. However, they tend to cool down quickly. They are champions of independence and freedom, and are outspoken with their opinions. They are capable of quick action and getting things done in a hurry. Red may be a favorite color.

Appearance: Aries Ascending tends toward better than average height, spare body, rather elongated face and neck. The complexion is frequently ruddy; the hair is often red or sandy in color. The frontal area of the head is usually pronounced. The eyebrows may be heavy and tend to bridge the nose. The forehead may be wide and the chin pointed. It is likely that there may be scars or marks about the head. The Adam's apple may protrude.

Taurus Ascending

Taurus rules the throat. Therefore, it is expected that Taurus Ascending would emphasize this area. There may be a talent or at least a strong interest in singing and speaking. The throat also has to do with the appetite. There is likely to be an emphasis on satisfying the "appetites" of the body. These individuals are endowed with great self-reliance, generally easy-going, but possess a strongly persistent and determined nature. Taurus Ascending is highly attuned to practical and material matters — money and possessions. Basically kind and loving, but inclined to be frequently stubborn and jealous. They greatly enjoy the seeking of pleasure. Tempers are not easily aroused, but they can be violent if pushed too far. They are usually patient and willing to wait for their projects to succeed.

Appearance: Taurus Ascending normally gives a solid, hard body of average height. There is a tendency toward plumpness, especially of the torso. Usually the face is square, the neck rather short and strong. There is a general fullness to all the facial features. The eyes may be prominent or slightly protruding. The hair tends toward the lighter shades of brown. Shoulders may be wide and square; chest thick. The nostrils may be flared, especially when angered. Hands are "pudgy."

Gemini Ascending

Gemini is ruled by Mercury, the God of Speed. Consequently, Gemini Ascending tends to make the native quick, and quick witted. Further, Gemini controls the hands, arms, and nervous system generally, so the individual is likely to be interested in using the hands as well as the mind. This ascendant gives a probing, curious mind which is constantly alert for anything new or different. There is a continuing desire to acquire knowledge and to experiment. The individual feels a great need to communicate verbally and/or with the written word. The individual is of a dual nature, and may have income from more than one source. The mental and mechanical aptitudes are usually good and about equal. Gemini Ascending should guard against being a "jack-of-all-trades" only and develop more persistence.

Appearance: Normally Gemini Ascending causes the individual to be slender, erect, and often of average or less than average height. The legs frequently are "bird-like." There is seldom an overweight problem with this ascendant. The body is best described as wiry. The arms and fingers tend to be rather long and thin. The face seems to be "double" — there may be a cleft in the chin and even the nose, which may tend to be slightly hooked and reddish. Hair may be dark brown.

Cancer Ascending

Cancer, whose ruler is the Moon, rules the stomach — the holder and collector of that which sustains life (a point and source of pleasure and comfort). Emotions and feelings play a major role in this ascendant's mode of living. There is acute sensitivity to all persons and conditions nearby. There is a fertile imagination, sentimentality, and a sympathetic and talkative nature. There is normally a great fondness for the home, mother, and sometimes the father. Cancer Ascending tends to give an emotional nature and extreme sensitivity to criticism. They love the past, the fireside, a good cigar, mom, apple pie, the kitchen, and everything that smacks of tradition. With this ascendant, the individual will make a practice of "collecting" either material things, personalities, or experiences.

Appearance: Cancer Ascendants are often nicely curved. Adults usually have broad hips and put on weight easily in that area. Height is normally short to medium. The arms (which may have crab-like positions and motions) and legs tend to be short and stocky. Feet and hands are small and rather delicate. There may be a rather undulating gait to the walk. The face is usually round — Moon-shaped — and the profile may be "dished" as the Moon appears when not full.

Leo Ascending

Leo's ruler is the Sun. In Astrology, the Sun rules the heart and the basic individuality. Leo Ascending makes for a bright and shining disposition, and a strong individuality. There is a magnetic personal appeal that begets admiration — what Leo most wants. The individual is normally good natured and generous — sometimes overly so. Inclined to speak frankly, loudly, and with a flair that stimulates listeners to buy or believe. Leo Ascending is demonstrative, energetic, and possessed of great energy. There is a burning desire and need to be the center of attention, to "show-off." The individual is basically good natured, popular, generous, and of a rather regal disposition. There is a tendency to desire to "run" the lives of friends. Generally, these are the "back-slappers" and "hand-shakers" of the Zodiac.

Appearance: Leo Ascending is normally tall, broad shouldered and large framed. There is a strong tendency to put on weight after a streamlined youth. Often the hair is "sunshine bright." The smile is broad and beaming. The brisk walk and carriage is regal — full of pride and dignity — perhaps pompous at times. Sometimes the hair grows low and heavy on the neck, much like the lion. Everything about the face seems to be "generous" in size and proportion.

Virgo Ascending

Virgo, like Gemini, is ruled by Mercury, which makes the Virgo Ascendant also a "Mercurial" (mental) individual. Virgo rules the lower intestinal tract, which assimilates food for the body. Virgo Ascending is constantly assimilating, evaluating, criticizing food for the mind. There is a liking for work, but an undue amount of worry over perfection in the work that is done. This ascendant endows a self-critical attitude which tends to modesty and a feeling of inferiority. The individual is basically conservative, diplomatic, tactful, and high-strung. There is a good amount of shrewdness, and a strong desire for money. Virgo Ascending learns readily and quickly, and has a deep desire to tell others how to improve themselves. They are inclined to "tell it like it is" even when it would be better not to do so.

Appearance: Virgo Ascending tends to average height, average weight, and an angular but good build. The shoulders and hips are fairly wide. It is relatively easy to put on weight. Facial features are usually small but nicely shaped. The nose may be slightly hooked. The complexion is fair and smooth. The bone structure of the face usually makes this ascendant quite photogenic. The walk is smooth and graceful. The general appearance could be described as "clean-cut."

Libra Ascending

Venus (Goddess of Beauty) rules Libra. Libra rules the kidneys and lower back. The kidneys, through their elimination of wastes and poisons from the body, tend to maintain balance and harmony. So, Libra Ascending is concerned with "maintaining balance" in the affairs of mankind. This ascendant is a lover of beauty and order and constantly seeks to bring harmony and balance into their lives and into the lives of friends. There is an inclination toward "match-making," party-giving, and party-going. A great interest in "justice for all." Libra Ascending prefers the "good" life, surrounded with all that is beautiful in color, symmetry, and in proper taste. Libra Ascending makes for a courteous, pleasant, and agreeable person. Sometimes there may be a tendency to "meddle." Frequently this ascendant is the champion of the "underdog."

Appearance: Normally the body is well-formed, tall, slender, and inclined to stoutness in middle age. The hair is well-kept, and usually very dark or black in color. Because of the Venus rulership, many Libra Ascendants can be termed "beautiful" in appearance. Features are usually nicely shaped, the teeth may be "pearly," the lips generous and finely chiseled. Frequently the hair is naturally curly. Generally there is a sort of "roundness" to all the features.

Scorpio Ascending

Mars, the God of War, rules Scorpio. Scorpio rules the "secrets," or organs of elimination and reproduction. This rulership gives the Scorpio Ascendant an intense drive and desire to do away with whatever stands in the way, and to produce, to generate results. Scorpio Ascending is good for success because of the strength, intenseness, drive, determination, and aggressiveness it gives the native. The ambition is powerful — sometimes too strong for the individual's own good. Scorpio Ascending is tenacious, determined, secretive, penetrating, critical, suspicious, emotional, and often blunt in speech and actions. They are quick-witted, alert, forceful, and seemingly fond of contest. Their purposes are accomplished if not by subtlety, then by strength of will, or force if necessary. Luxury is appreciated, but they can be very frugal if required to achieve their ends.

Appearance: The height is usually about average. Scorpio Ascending makes for a stout body and face which may appear "stuffed" or "puffy." The eyes are large and penetrating. They may be the outstanding feature of the face. The hair is nearly always black and rather thick and course, sometimes curly. The nose may be described as "Roman." The skin is frequently sallow and may be oily. The walk may be quick and "bouncy."

Sagittarius Ascending

Jupiter, called "The Great Benefic," rules Sagittarius. Sagittarius rules the thighs and hips. The thighs and hips are the prime movers in enabling man to travel afar, to stand, to sit, and enjoy life. Sagittarius Ascending causes the native to be jovial and hearty, a witty and adept conversationalist — capable of telling a "tall" story now and again. They have a somewhat uncanny ability to meet and become "old friends" with total strangers quickly, mainly because of their ability to make others feel important. This ascendant likes to travel, and likes the great out-of-doors in a physical or a mental sense. There is a strong desire for freedom of thought and action. They are frank and honest to the letter. Also inclined to be somewhat impatient and impulsive, which may cause frequent changes of interests. They like things done on a grand scale.

Appearance: "Distinguished looking" is a term which will describe many with Sagittarius Ascending. The native may be rather tall and large, however, not overweight until middle age. The face tends to be roundish and jovial, somewhat elongated. The teeth may be large and can protrude slightly. The hair is dark in youth, but impressively white in later years. There is frequently a tendency to stamp or scrape the feet.

Capricorn Ascending

Saturn, the "Taskmaster" rules Capricorn. Capricorn rules the knees — which enable man to raise himself to his maximum height, but which are also subject to bending quickly and are quite vulnerable to blows and injury. Capricorn Ascending inclines the native toward a "saturnine" personality — serious, gloomy, heavy, grave. There is much practicality, cautiousness, and prudence in all actions. The individual is status and success oriented, and never fails to use whatever is near as the attempt to climb higher up the ladder is made. Capricorn Ascending is basically an "opportunist," constantly striving, frequently failing, but always persisting in climbing to higher levels in life. This ascendant may cause the native to appear cold, and snobbish at times. Sometimes a sense of humor is almost totally concealed. Capricorn Ascending is highly practical.

Appearance: The stature is average, but more times than not shorter than average. The chest is usually flat, and the body in general tends toward being lean, except for the legs which more likely than not will be heavy. Ankles frequently are thick. The features may be rather small and sharp. Oftentimes the skin and hair will be darker than other members of the same family not having Capricorn Ascending. The hair is very dark, usually black.

Aquarius Ascending

Uranus, the planet of "Sudden Changes," rules Aquarius. Aquarius rules the calves and ankles of the legs which are subject to many changes as man progresses forward and walks — even on the Moon. Basically the Aquarius Ascending native is kind, sociable, original, tolerant, broad-minded about most things, and intellectual. There is much curiosity and delving into the occult and the "off-beat" areas of life. This ascendant may cause the native to be regarded by many as eccentric in one or more ways. Aquarius Ascending wants attention and admiration from a wide circle of friends. The individual may smile a lot, but seldom laughs aloud. The general manner is abrupt. There is more than a passing interest in wide-scale reform for the benefit of mankind.

Appearance: Aquarius Ascending usually gives what might be called a "striking" appearance. Height tends to be average to above average. The build is full or square in most respects. The waist may be long; shoulders square. The features are usually even and "handsome." The chin may be strong and pointed. Aquarius Ascending probably has a very excellent profile. The walk may be sudden and eccentric — like the thinking processes.

Pisces Ascending

Neptune, "Ruler of the Waters," rules Pisces. Pisces rules the feet. As the feet are sometimes uncertain which is the next step, or which way to turn, so is Pisces Ascending. This ascendant gives the native a high-voltage emotional nature and a dreamy, imaginative, sensitive, and intellectually creative nature. Pisces Ascending tends to get along well with all types of people until let down or disappointed in some way. Secrets are enjoyed. There is subtlety and non-aggressiveness in the approach Pisces Ascending makes to others, and to life in general. There is a strong tendency toward indecisiveness, and they frequently "beat about the bush" when confronted with the need to decide and to act. Pisces Ascending is idealistic, impressionable, apt in detail and orderly in manner. Feelings run very deep.

Appearance: Pisces Ascending tends to be relatively small and well-proportioned. They may put on weight later in life. Arms and legs usually are short; hands may be small and "artistic." This ascendant tends to give large dreamy eyes and long, thick lashes. The mouth may be soft and sensitive; the nose small and well-formed. There is a tendency toward a double chin, or even a triple chin if overweight. The feet may be unusual in some way.

The Moon -- Your Mentality

Without the Moon, nights would be dark. The Moon in your Horoscope represents instinct and habit, feeling, memory, imagination, receptivity, impressionability, the desire for new experience, the domestic and protective instincts and impulses. While the Sun represents the Conscious Mind, the Moon represents the Subconscious Mind. The Moon's action is to synthesize, to understand. In short, the Moon in your Horoscope is your Mentality (not I.Q.) — the methods and processes through which you go in presenting your Individuality (your Sun) to the world through your Personality (your Ascendant).

MOON IN ARIES

The Moon placed here stresses independence, drive, self-assertiveness, a headstrong attitude, push, great energy, impulsiveness, enthusiasm, inventiveness and originality. The native may be easy to anger; self-reliant; demand authority and become militantly aggressive. There is indicated conflicts with parents, teachers, and those in command. The senses are clear and quick; the tongue is sharp; the temper may be violent; the mind is active. The desire for success is great.

MOON IN TAURUS

The Moon here emphasizes the materialistic — the emphasis is on possessions. The native collects. There is a passionate desire for attention, and a fond longing for all the things that make for the "good life." Moon in Taurus inclines toward indolence, self indulgence, romance, conservatism in many areas, and a strong desire for material success. The individual is sociable, sensual, determined (stubborn), persistent, slow moving but sure mentally. This placement makes for stability.

MOON IN GEMINI

The Gemini Moon makes the native mentally alert, self-expressive, talkative, adaptable, versatile, perceptive, flexible, nervous, articulate, curious, changeable, intelligent, charming, witty, shrewd, restless, and frequently ambidextrous. To this native, "variety is the spice of life." The ability to learn rapidly is common. The Moon here often lacks depth, making the native seem superficial. There may also be a marked lack of perseverance. The sense of humor is highly developed.

MOON IN CANCER

Cancer is the sign of the Zodiac ruled by the Moon. Placement here makes the characteristics mentioned doubly strong. This native seeks security, comfort, recognition, and acceptance. They are highly emotional and sensitive, creative, given to brooding, selfishness, and self-satisfaction. These natives are inclined to be suspicious by nature, loyal to traditions — home, mother, country. They love ease and comfort. Not highly active, but passively aggressive.

MOON IN LEO

This placement of the Moon tends to uplift the native socially and mentally and places him in positions of trust, respect, and responsibility, normally. The individual may be noble in thoughts and actions, and filled with drive, confidence, ambition, and a desire to lead. The native is confident, fiery, dashing, honorable, generous, proud, straightforward, idealistic, and dignified. There is a strong love for luxury, and a desire for social pomp and prominence. This is a good placement usually.

MOON IN VIRGO

The Virgo Moon causes the native to utilize the intellectual, rather than the emotional approach to most matters. The Virgo Moon may be discriminating, fussy, analytical, honest, persistent, trustworthy, judicious, loyal, confident, industrious, and hard-working. Further, there is reserve, fastidiousness, and practicality. This placement must constantly have a goal in order to be happy. This is the inquiring mind that not only wants to see what makes things "tick," but why they do so.

MOON IN LIBRA

The Moon in Libra causes the native to have an interest in public relations, advertising, law, and design. Normally the native is hospitable, friendly, tolerant, fond of people, gentle, elegant, understanding, and artistically inclined. There can be good success in partnerships of all kinds. There is a love for the refined, the luxurious. Generally, the nature is affectionate and easily swayed. Sometimes there is too much reliance on others to make important decisions. The Moon here can lead to general indecisiveness.

MOON IN SCORPIO

Moon in Scorpio natives are intense, dynamic, self-reliant, serious, penetrating, energetic, abrupt, impulsive, virile, emotional, outspoken, vindictive, determined, highly sexed, magnetic, shrewd, and occult-oriented. There is a deep interest in the mysterious and unknown; there may be extremes with the passions — there is a strong attraction for the opposite sex. The Scorpio Moon thinks for itself — it will not be pushed. This Moon is capable of good success when desire is great.

MOON IN SAGITTARIUS

The Sagittarius Moon reflects the native who is outspoken, buoyant, interested in learning and spreading knowledge. There is love for adventure and travel, whether in fact or mentally. This native is frank, generous, charming, imaginative, unorthodox, restless, sincere, candid, and dual-natured. This restlessness may bring about many changes of residence, or changes of mind. There is an interest in reading, writing, publishing, advertising, and publicity.

MOON IN CAPRICORN

The native with a Capricorn Moon is earthy, materialistic, ambitious, status conscious, self-conscious, stubborn, determined, emotionally conservative, easily depressed, cold, desirous of power and position, practical, steadfast, reliable, serious, prudent, capricious, and tends too often to look on the dark side of matters. They are hard workers, and will persist almost forever to achieve a goal. They possess executive ability and are capable of management.

MOON IN AQUARIUS

The Moon in Aquarius highlights the unusual, the "different." The Aquarius Moon is an advanced thinker, generous, broad-minded, humane, stubborn, unconventional, intuitive, imaginative, eccentric, highly idealistic, liberal, scientific, broadly sympathetic, but frequently somewhat impractical. This Moon loves recognition and admiration; consequently, it seeks flattery, and often flatters others. The interest in others is more on a universal level, rather than a personal one.

MOON IN PISCES

A Pisces Moon tends to make the native restless, sensitive, impressionable, moody, self-indulgent, perceptive, easily hurt, fascinated by the occult, psychic, lacking in self-confidence, dreamy, emotional, undependable at times, changeable, intemperate, romantic, sentimental, gentle, passive, and overly-optimistic. The Pisces Moon is frequently late for appointments. There is a tendency to look at the world through rose-colored glasses. Fond of travel, especially over water.

Sun In Houses

SUN IN 1st HOUSE

The Sun placed here tends to give the native a bright, "sunny" disposition. There is great emphasis on the self. This individual usually puts on a good "front" — frank, upright, dignified, egotistical at times, prominent. There are good recuperative powers normally. This placement inclines toward a strong personality.

SUN IN 2nd HOUSE

A favorable Sun placement. The overall personality is integrated where needs are concerned. The native is able to distinguish between whims and necessity. This placement often "attracts" money. The native is ambitious. Money comes and goes easily. There is a tendency to treasure the possessions and material things in life.

SUN IN 3rd HOUSE

This Sun tends to attract "bright" people to the native. There is usually considerable contact with intelligent, creative persons, There is generally an optimistic outlook on life. There may be extensive travel and moving about. There is a general predisposition for the native to make decisions at the right times.

SUN IN 4th HOUSE

Usually favorable for making money in real estate and from the land. This Sun is indicative of one who can be ecstatic where the home and family are concerned. Indeed, this may be the dreamer who allows the world to pass unnoticed. This Sun indicates favorable connections with parents, and ultimate security, perhaps through them.

SUN IN 5th HOUSE

A very good indicator for success. There may be a tendency to dominate others in the affairs of the heart. This native has the ability to make loved ones happy in a physical sense. There is usually acceptance and popularity, adulation, and success with members of the opposite sex. The native may tend to be self-indulgent.

SUN IN 6th HOUSE

A 6th House Sun is the basic story of unfaltering determination. There is a high degree of faithfulness; a deep regard for health, beauty, and vitality. Extreme pride in achievement and a desire for appreciation for all services rendered. The native could be somewhat vain. There is an ambition to serve; and an interest in hygiene.

SUN IN 7th HOUSE

The Sun here is "pleasant" in that the native tends to attract others to himself. Often he can bring happiness and good fortune to partnerships. There is interest and pride in relationships of all kinds. The native may be an "opportunist." May be deeply loved or bitterly hated — there is little "middle ground." Ambitious plans.

SUN IN 8th HOUSE

This is a powerful location for the Sun which gives the native bountiful amounts of creative energy. An outlet should be found, possibly acting or writing. This Sun tends to brighten an otherwise "dark corner" of the Zodiac. It can bring the native a bright, perhaps humorous outlook on money matters. Intent on improvement.

SUN IN 9th HOUSE

This Sun tells of lofty and noble motives, but the sense of practicality may be somewhat lacking. Indeed, the sense of high ideals may even, at times, border on the fanatical. Generally, there is broad wisdom, a love for travel, and there may be foreign journeys. This travel could well be done in the normal line of business.

SUN IN 10th HOUSE

A 10th House Sun frequently brings the native fame, often at an early age. This native is strongly self-conscious and determined to achieve and to succeed. He may occupy a high position, and may be able to garner a lot of public support and sympathy for himself and/or his "cause." A favorable position for "stardom."

SUN IN 11th HOUSE

This positioning tends to give the native a strong appeal to the opposite sex. There may also be a tendency to attract "celebrities." The native prides himself generally in "right thoughts" and "right friends." Hopes and wishes become challenges, and, unless fulfilled, the native may be inclined to brood.

SUN IN 12th HOUSE

This Sun has a tendency to idealize the sexual state of affairs. There is a search for his own type of perfection. Needs to learn some of the truths and actualities of life, and that others have ordeals in life as well. Success is indicated. There may be eccentricities — native may prefer seclusion, secrecy.

Moon In Houses

MOON IN 1st HOUSE

A 1st House Moon inclines the native toward general moodiness and procrastination. There is a knack for dealing successfully with women. There is a consciousness of the personal appearance which can be capitalized upon. The native is responsive to public reaction. Subject to quick changes in mood, and restlessness.

MOON IN 2nd HOUSE

This Moon may incline the native to embrace superficial values. There is a tendency to be attracted to bright and shiny objects and people. The thoughts generally are of obtaining rather than of multiplying or expanding. Wealth comes through appealing to public imagination. Native attracts publicity, even notoriety.

MOON IN 3rd HOUSE

The 3rd House Moon can cause the native to be full of doubts, but it tends to promote a rather healthy intellectual curiosity for mental growth. There is a propensity to take chances often. This placement makes for a generally intriguing and rather mysterious personality. A good memory and desire for variety are typical.

MOON IN 4th HOUSE

This Moon stresses loyalty to the family, the land, and the country. The native genuinely enjoys making a place for those loved. Good for a sense of humor. Unfortunately, the native, at times seems to be playing a role which may make him appear ridiculous. Indications of comfort in old age. Mother is a strong influence.

MOON IN 5th HOUSE

This Moon often brings early success and publicity. Often the native may make a "big splash" which may not last. There is an excellent sense of the dramatic. There tends to be a constant search for pleasure. Also, there is a tendency to "speculate" in matters of the heart. May be poetically romantic. Love affairs may be numerous.

MOON IN 6th HOUSE

This Moon is indicative of a restless nature and numerous job changes. There may be much indecision in connection with the profession. The native is highly interested in techniques — the "how and why" of the way things work. The native is apt to give the impression of being "cranky" to those who work with and for him.

MOON IN 7th HOUSE

A 7th House Moon represents popularity with the public. The native is better at "smoothing over" than at initiating endeavors. There are many opportunities to marry, but the native needs to develop more stability. Tendency to attract persons of great sensitivity, and who seek more permanence and dedication than he may offer.

MOON IN 8th HOUSE

This Moon emphasizes the feeling that security is of utmost importance. There is a saving instinct — for the future. He invests, but may complain that others have all the fun. There is self-denial out of a sense of duty. Women investors are easily attracted. There may be an interest in what may be termed the "morbid."

MOON IN 9th HOUSE

This placement is the receptive, imaginative mind — the mind of the dreamer, the creator, the artist, the individual who often may seem about "six inches away from reality." There could be a tendency to relate experiences and ideas rather abstractly. The beliefs (even superstitions) are sincere. Mind changes are frequent.

MOON IN 10th HOUSE

This position of the Moon is indicative of changes where goals and the profession are concerned. This native is usually "in touch with the people," — is normally able to "feel the pulse" of the public. This placement is good for publicity, advertising, and promotion — even exploitation, particularly of females.

MOON IN 11th HOUSE

This Moon reflects the fact that much of the native's security depends upon friends, and the hopes and wishes he creates for himself. Popularity varies from time to time, and from group to group. Desires more loyalty than he sometimes offers. There may be many acquaintances, but not many really close friends.

MOON IN 12th HOUSE

The Moon here is good for publicity in connection with all types of institutions — hospitals, prisons, etc. There is over-sensitivity about his background, family, friends. The native can be extremely provincial. There may be fears connected with travel on strange ground. Should learn moods can be turned to creativity.

The Aspects

Certain angular distances between the Sun and Moon tend to modify — change, strengthen, or weaken — the characteristic readings for the native so that he may not totally fit the exact Astrological delineation given in Astrology Dial-A-Scope. If, in reading a Chart, you find the native to be quite different than the normal descriptions given, you should consider the Aspects in the Chart.

Aspects are divided into two classes — harmonious and inharmonious. In considering Aspects, remember these basic facts:

1) Each Sign of the Zodiac is 30 degrees wide.
2) Fire (Signs) combine well with Air (Signs), but not with Water (Signs) or Earth (Signs).
3) Water (Signs) combine with Earth (Signs), but not with Fire (Signs) or Air (Signs).

FAVORABLE

The harmonious (favorable) aspects tend to emphasize the more positive and constructive qualities of the Sun and/or Moon in the Houses. The favorable aspects are:

☌ **Conjunction:** Planets in the same House or Sign. *(Example:* Sun and Moon both in Aries, or both in any one of the other 11 Signs.)

△ **Trine:** Sun and Moon 120 degrees apart (4 Signs away). *(Example:* Sun (or Moon) in Aries, Moon (or Sun) either in Leo or Sagittarius.)

✶ **Sextile:** Sun and Moon 60 degrees apart (2 Signs away). *(Example:* Sun (or Moon) in Aries, Moon (or Sun) either in Gemini or Aquarius.)

⋎ **Semi-sextile:** Sun and Moon 30 degrees apart (1 Sign away). *(Example:* Sun (or Moon) in Aries, Moon (or Sun) either in Taurus or Pisces.)

UNFAVORABLE

The inharmonious (unfavorable) aspects tend to emphasize the more negative and destructive characteristics of the Sun and/or Moon in the Houses. The unfavorable aspects are:

☍ **Opposition:** Sun and Moon 180 degrees apart (6 Signs away). *(Example:* Sun (or Moon) in Aries, Moon (or Sun) in Libra.)

□ **Square:** Sun and Moon 90 degrees apart (3 Signs away). *(Example:* Sun (or Moon) in Aries, Moon (or Sun) either in Cancer or Capricorn.)

The Elbert Wade

Moon Tables

(1900 – 1980)

The following pages contain tables which will enable you to determine the Moon's Sign placement for any day of any year from 1900 to 1980 inclusive.

These tables indicate the DAY on which the Moon changed from one Sign to the next. The Moon moves in regular order from Aries to Taurus, to Gemini, to Cancer, to Leo, to Virgo, to Libra, to Scorpio, to Sagittarius, to Capricorn, to Aquarius, to Pisces.

Since the Moon's motion through the Signs is not always constant, it is not possible here to indicate the exact hour, minute, and second the Moon changed signs.

Normally, the Moon remains in each of the 12 Signs for 2.33 days. It makes its complete transit through the 12 Signs each 28 days (a Lunar month), but its daily motion varies from 12 degrees to 15 degrees through this 28 day cycle. No doubt this is why Shakespeare speaks of the "inconstant" Moon.

TO FIND CORRECT MOON SIGN

1. Find the YEAR of birth in the right margin on the pages that follow.
2. Move left to the MONTH of birth.
3. Move down to find the DAY. (See Examples 1 & 2 below.)
4. Determine the Moon Sign by reading the abbreviation to the right of DAY.

Ari	— Aries	Lib	— Libra
Tau	— Taurus	Sco	— Scorpio
Gem	— Gemini	Sag	— Sagittarius
Can	— Cancer	Cap	— Capricorn
Leo	— Leo	Aqu	— Aquarius
Vir	— Virgo	Pis	— Pisces

Example 1: For a December 31, 1900 birth. Turn to next page. Note Moon entered Tau (Taurus) on December 30, 1900. Checking January 1901, note Moon entered Gem (Gemini) January 1, 1901. Therefore, the Moon is clearly in Taurus. The Moon indicator on Dial-A-Scope should be set for Taurus.

Example 2: For a January 1, 1901 birth. Since the Moon entered Gemini on January 1st (exact hour not known), it is possible that the Moon could be either in Taurus or Gemini. If birth hour is prior to Noon, it is probable that the Moon was in Taurus. If after Noon, the Moon Sign is likely Gemini. To find out, first read the Taurus Moon and House placement descriptions in this book. If the reading does not fit the individual, then you know that Gemini is the proper Moon Sign. Set Dial-A-Scope for a Gemini Moon and read the appropriate descriptions. With a little practice, you will determine proper settings quickly and without question.

1900

JAN.	FEB.	MAR.	APR.	MAY	JUN.	JUL.	AUG.	SEP.	OCT.	NOV.	DEC.
2 Aqu	1 Pis	2 Ari	1 Tau	2 Can	1 Leo	1 Vir	2 Sco	1 Sag	1 Cap	1 Pis	1 Ari
4 Pis	3 Ari	4 Tau	3 Gem	5 Leo	4 Vir	3 Lib	5 Sag	3 Cap	3 Aqu	4 Ari	3 Tau
6 Ari	5 Tau	6 Gem	5 Can	7 Vir	6 Lib	6 Sco	7 Cap	6 Aqu	5 Pis	6 Tau	5 Gem
9 Tau	7 Gem	8 Can	7 Leo	10 Lib	9 Sco	8 Sag	9 Aqu	8 Pis	7 Ari	8 Gem	7 Can
11 Gem	9 Can	11 Leo	10 Vir	12 Sco	11 Sag	11 Cap	11 Pis	10 Ari	9 Tau	10 Can	9 Leo
13 Can	12 Leo	14 Vir	12 Lib	15 Sag	13 Cap	13 Aqu	13 Ari	12 Tau	11 Gem	12 Leo	12 Vir
16 Leo	14 Vir	16 Lib	15 Sco	17 Cap	15 Aqu	15 Pis	15 Tau	14 Gem	13 Can	14 Vir	14 Lib
18 Vir	17 Lib	19 Sco	17 Sag	19 Aqu	18 Pis	17 Ari	17 Gem	16 Can	16 Leo	17 Lib	17 Sco
21 Lib	19 Sco	21 Sag	20 Cap	21 Pis	20 Ari	19 Tau	20 Leo	18 Leo	18 Vir	19 Sco	19 Sag
23 Sco	22 Sag	23 Cap	22 Aqu	23 Ari	22 Tau	21 Gem	22 Leo	21 Vir	21 Lib	22 Sag	22 Cap
26 Sag	24 Cap	26 Aqu	24 Pis	26 Tau	24 Gem	23 Can	25 Vir	23 Lib	23 Sco	24 Cap	24 Aqu
28 Cap	26 Aqu	28 Pis	26 Ari	28 Gem	26 Can	26 Leo	27 Lib	26 Sco	26 Sag	27 Aqu	26 Pis
30 Aqu	28 Pis	30 Ari	28 Tau	30 Can	29 Leo	28 Vir	30 Sco	28 Sag	28 Cap	29 Pis	28 Ari
			30 Gem			31 Lib			30 Aqu		30 Tau

1901

JAN.	FEB.	MAR.	APR.	MAY	JUN.	JUL.	AUG.	SEP.	OCT.	NOV.	DEC.
1 Gem	2 Leo	1 Leo	2 Lib	2 Sco	1 Sag	1 Cap	2 Pis	2 Tau	1 Gem	2 Leo	2 Vir
3 Can	4 Vir	4 Vir	5 Sco	5 Sag	3 Cap	3 Aqu	4 Ari	4 Gem	4 Can	4 Vir	4 Lib
6 Leo	7 Lib	6 Lib	7 Sag	7 Cap	6 Aqu	5 Pis	6 Tau	6 Can	6 Leo	7 Lib	7 Sco
8 Vir	9 Sco	9 Sco	10 Cap	10 Aqu	8 Pis	7 Ari	8 Gem	9 Leo	8 Vir	9 Sco	9 Sag
11 Lib	12 Sag	11 Sag	12 Aqu	12 Pis	10 Ari	10 Tau	10 Can	11 Vir	11 Lib	12 Sag	12 Cap
13 Sco	14 Cap	14 Cap	14 Pis	14 Ari	12 Tau	12 Gem	12 Leo	13 Lib	13 Sco	14 Cap	14 Aqu
16 Sag	17 Aqu	16 Aqu	17 Ari	16 Tau	14 Gem	14 Can	15 Vir	16 Sco	16 Sag	17 Aqu	16 Pis
18 Cap	19 Pis	18 Pis	19 Tau	18 Gem	16 Can	16 Leo	17 Lib	18 Sag	18 Cap	19 Pis	19 Ari
20 Aqu	21 Ari	20 Ari	21 Gem	20 Can	19 Leo	18 Vir	19 Sco	21 Cap	21 Aqu	21 Ari	21 Tau
22 Pis	23 Tau	22 Tau	23 Can	22 Leo	21 Vir	21 Lib	22 Sag	23 Aqu	23 Pis	23 Tau	23 Gem
24 Ari	25 Gem	24 Gem	25 Leo	24 Vir	23 Lib	23 Sco	24 Cap	25 Pis	25 Ari	25 Gem	25 Can
26 Tau	27 Can	26 Can	27 Vir	27 Lib	26 Sco	26 Sag	27 Aqu	27 Ari	27 Tau	27 Can	27 Leo
29 Gem		29 Leo	30 Lib	29 Sco	28 Sag	28 Cap	29 Pis	29 Tau	29 Gem	29 Leo	29 Vir
31 Can		31 Vir				30 Aqu	31 Ari		31 Can		31 Lib

38

1902

JAN.	FEB.	MAR.	APR.	MAY	JUN.	JUL.	AUG.	SEP.	OCT.	NOV.	DEC.
3 Sco	2 Sag	1 Sag	2 Aqu	2 Pis	1 Ari	2 Gem	1 Can	1 Vir	1 Lib	2 Sag	2 Cap
5 Sag	4 Cap	4 Cap	5 Pis	4 Ari	3 Tau	4 Can	3 Leo	3 Lib	3 Sco	4 Cap	4 Aqu
8 Cap	7 Aqu	6 Aqu	7 Ari	6 Tau	5 Gem	6 Leo	5 Vir	6 Sco	5 Sag	7 Aqu	7 Pis
10 Aqu	9 Pis	8 Pis	9 Tau	8 Gem	7 Can	8 Vir	7 Lib	8 Sag	8 Cap	9 Pis	9 Ari
13 Pis	11 Ari	10 Ari	11 Gem	10 Can	9 Leo	11 Lib	9 Sco	11 Cap	10 Aqu	12 Ari	11 Tau
15 Ari	13 Tau	13 Tau	13 Can	12 Leo	11 Vir	13 Sco	12 Sag	13 Aqu	13 Pis	14 Tau	13 Gem
17 Tau	15 Gem	15 Gem	15 Leo	15 Vir	13 Lib	15 Sag	14 Cap	15 Pis	15 Ari	16 Gem	15 Can
19 Gem	18 Can	17 Can	17 Vir	17 Lib	16 Sco	18 Cap	17 Aqu	18 Ari	17 Tau	18 Can	17 Leo
21 Can	20 Leo	19 Leo	20 Lib	19 Sco	18 Sag	20 Aqu	19 Pis	20 Tau	19 Gem	20 Leo	19 Vir
23 Leo	22 Vir	21 Vir	22 Sco	22 Sag	21 Cap	23 Pis	21 Ari	22 Gem	21 Can	22 Vir	21 Lib
25 Vir	24 Lib	23 Lib	25 Sag	24 Cap	23 Aqu	25 Ari	24 Tau	24 Can	23 Leo	24 Lib	24 Sco
28 Lib	27 Sco	26 Sco	27 Cap	27 Aqu	26 Pis	27 Tau	26 Gem	26 Leo	26 Vir	27 Sco	26 Sag
30 Sco		28 Sag	30 Aqu	29 Pis	28 Ari	30 Gem	28 Can	28 Vir	28 Lib	29 Sag	29 Cap
		31 Cap			30 Tau		30 Leo		30 Sco		31 Aqu

1903

JAN.	FEB.	MAR.	APR.	MAY	JUN.	JUL.	AUG.	SEP.	OCT.	NOV.	DEC.
3 Pis	1 Ari	1 Ari	1 Gem	1 Can	1 Vir	1 Lib	2 Sag	3 Aqu	3 Pis	2 Ari	1 Tau
5 Ari	4 Tau	3 Tau	4 Can	3 Leo	3 Lib	3 Sco	4 Cap	5 Pis	5 Ari	4 Tau	3 Gem
8 Tau	6 Gem	5 Gem	6 Leo	5 Vir	6 Sco	5 Sag	7 Aqu	8 Ari	8 Tau	6 Gem	6 Can
10 Gem	8 Can	7 Can	8 Vir	7 Lib	8 Sag	8 Cap	9 Pis	10 Tau	10 Gem	8 Can	8 Leo
12 Can	10 Leo	10 Leo	10 Lib	10 Sco	11 Cap	10 Aqu	12 Ari	13 Gem	12 Can	10 Leo	10 Vir
14 Leo	12 Vir	11 Vir	12 Sco	12 Sag	13 Aqu	13 Pis	14 Tau	15 Can	14 Leo	12 Vir	12 Lib
16 Vir	14 Lib	14 Lib	15 Sag	14 Cap	16 Pis	15 Ari	16 Gem	17 Leo	16 Vir	15 Lib	14 Sco
18 Lib	16 Sco	16 Sco	17 Cap	17 Aqu	18 Ari	18 Tau	18 Can	19 Vir	18 Lib	17 Sco	16 Sag
20 Sco	19 Sag	18 Sag	20 Aqu	19 Pis	20 Tau	20 Gem	20 Leo	21 Lib	20 Sco	19 Sag	19 Cap
23 Sag	21 Cap	21 Cap	22 Pis	22 Ari	23 Gem	22 Can	22 Vir	23 Sco	23 Sag	21 Cap	21 Aqu
25 Cap	24 Aqu	23 Aqu	24 Ari	24 Tau	25 Can	24 Leo	24 Lib	25 Sag	25 Cap	24 Aqu	24 Pis
28 Aqu	26 Pis	26 Pis	27 Tau	26 Gem	27 Leo	26 Vir	27 Sco	28 Cap	28 Aqu	26 Pis	26 Ari
30 Pis		28 Ari	29 Gem	28 Can	29 Vir	28 Lib	29 Sag	30 Aqu	30 Pis	29 Ari	29 Tau
		30 Tau		30 Leo		30 Sco	31 Cap				31 Gem

1904

JAN.	FEB.	MAR.	APR.	MAY	JUN.	JUL.	AUG.	SEP.	OCT.	NOV.	DEC.
2 Can	2 Vir	1 Vir	1 Sco	1 Sag	2 Aqu	2 Pis	1 Ari	2 Gem	1 Can	2 Vir	1 Lib
4 Leo	4 Lib	3 Lib	4 Sag	3 Cap	4 Pis	4 Ari	3 Tau	4 Can	4 Leo	4 Lib	4 Sco
6 Vir	7 Sco	5 Sco	6 Cap	6 Aqu	7 Ari	7 Tau	6 Gem	6 Leo	6 Vir	6 Sco	6 Sag
8 Lib	9 Sag	7 Sag	8 Aqu	8 Pis	9 Tau	9 Gem	8 Can	8 Vir	8 Lib	8 Sag	8 Cap
10 Sco	11 Cap	10 Cap	11 Pis	11 Ari	12 Gem	11 Can	10 Leo	10 Lib	10 Sco	10 Cap	10 Aqu
13 Sag	14 Aqu	12 Aqu	13 Ari	13 Tau	14 Can	13 Leo	12 Vir	12 Sco	12 Sag	13 Aqu	13 Pis
15 Cap	16 Pis	15 Pis	16 Tau	15 Gem	16 Leo	15 Vir	14 Lib	14 Sag	14 Cap	15 Pis	15 Ari
17 Aqu	19 Ari	17 Ari	18 Gem	18 Can	18 Vir	17 Lib	16 Sco	17 Cap	16 Aqu	18 Ari	18 Tau
20 Pis	21 Tau	20 Tau	20 Can	20 Leo	20 Lib	20 Sco	18 Sag	19 Aqu	19 Pis	20 Tau	20 Gem
23 Ari	24 Gem	22 Gem	23 Leo	22 Vir	22 Sco	22 Sag	20 Cap	22 Pis	21 Ari	23 Gem	22 Can
25 Tau	26 Can	24 Can	25 Vir	24 Lib	25 Sag	24 Cap	23 Aqu	24 Ari	24 Tau	25 Can	24 Leo
27 Gem	28 Leo	26 Leo	27 Lib	26 Sco	27 Cap	27 Aqu	25 Pis	27 Tau	26 Gem	27 Leo	26 Vir
29 Can		28 Vir	29 Sco	28 Sag	29 Aqu	29 Pis	28 Ari	29 Gem	29 Can	29 Vir	29 Lib
31 Leo		30 Lib		31 Cap			31 Tau		31 Leo		31 Sco

1905

JAN.	FEB.	MAR.	APR.	MAY	JUN.	JUL.	AUG.	SEP.	OCT.	NOV.	DEC.
2 Sag	3 Aqu	2 Aqu	1 Pis	1 Ari	2 Gem	1 Can	2 Vir	1 Lib	2 Sag	1 Cap	2 Pis
4 Cap	5 Pis	4 Pis	3 Ari	3 Tau	4 Can	4 Leo	4 Lib	3 Sco	4 Cap	3 Aqu	5 Ari
6 Aqu	8 Ari	7 Ari	6 Tau	6 Gem	6 Leo	6 Vir	6 Sco	5 Sag	6 Aqu	5 Pis	7 Tau
9 Pis	10 Tau	10 Tau	8 Gem	8 Can	9 Vir	8 Lib	9 Sag	7 Cap	9 Pis	8 Ari	10 Gem
11 Ari	13 Gem	12 Gem	11 Can	10 Leo	11 Lib	10 Sco	11 Cap	9 Aqu	11 Ari	10 Tau	12 Can
14 Tau	15 Can	14 Can	13 Leo	12 Vir	13 Sco	12 Sag	13 Aqu	12 Pis	14 Tau	13 Gem	15 Leo
16 Gem	17 Leo	17 Leo	15 Vir	15 Lib	15 Sag	14 Cap	15 Pis	14 Ari	16 Gem	15 Can	17 Vir
19 Can	19 Vir	19 Vir	17 Lib	17 Sco	17 Cap	17 Aqu	18 Ari	17 Tau	19 Can	17 Leo	19 Lib
21 Leo	21 Lib	21 Lib	19 Sco	19 Sag	19 Aqu	19 Pis	20 Tau	19 Gem	21 Leo	20 Vir	21 Sco
23 Vir	23 Sco	23 Sco	21 Sag	21 Cap	22 Pis	21 Ari	23 Gem	22 Can	23 Vir	22 Lib	23 Sag
25 Lib	25 Sag	25 Sag	23 Cap	23 Aqu	24 Ari	24 Tau	25 Can	24 Leo	26 Lib	24 Sco	25 Cap
27 Sco	28 Cap	27 Cap	26 Aqu	25 Pis	27 Tau	26 Gem	27 Leo	26 Vir	28 Sco	26 Sag	28 Aqu
29 Sag		29 Aqu	28 Pis	28 Ari	29 Gem	29 Can	30 Vir	28 Lib	29 Sag	28 Cap	30 Pis
31 Cap				30 Tau		31 Leo		30 Sco		30 Aqu	

1906

JAN.	FEB.	MAR.	APR.	MAY	JUN.	JUL.	AUG.	SEP.	OCT.	NOV.	DEC.
1 Ari	3 Gem	2 Gem	1 Can	3 Vir	1 Lib	1 Sco	1 Cap	2 Pis	1 Ari	3 Gem	2 Can
4 Tau	5 Can	4 Can	3 Leo	5 Lib	3 Sco	3 Sag	3 Aqu	4 Ari	4 Tau	5 Can	5 Leo
6 Gem	7 Leo	7 Leo	5 Vir	7 Sco	5 Sag	5 Cap	5 Pis	6 Tau	6 Gem	8 Leo	7 Vir
9 Can	10 Vir	9 Vir	8 Lib	9 Sag	7 Cap	7 Aqu	8 Ari	9 Gem	9 Can	10 Vir	10 Lib
11 Leo	12 Lib	11 Lib	10 Sco	11 Cap	9 Aqu	9 Pis	10 Tau	11 Can	11 Leo	12 Lib	12 Sco
13 Vir	14 Sco	13 Sco	12 Sag	13 Aqu	12 Pis	11 Ari	13 Gem	14 Leo	14 Vir	14 Sco	14 Sag
15 Lib	16 Sag	15 Sag	14 Cap	15 Pis	14 Ari	14 Tau	15 Can	16 Vir	16 Lib	16 Sag	16 Cap
18 Sco	18 Cap	17 Cap	16 Aqu	18 Ari	16 Tau	16 Gem	18 Leo	18 Lib	18 Sco	18 Cap	18 Aqu
20 Sag	20 Aqu	20 Aqu	18 Pis	20 Tau	19 Gem	19 Can	20 Vir	20 Sco	20 Sag	20 Aqu	20 Pis
22 Cap	23 Pis	22 Pis	20 Ari	23 Gem	21 Can	21 Leo	22 Lib	23 Sag	22 Cap	23 Pis	22 Ari
24 Aqu	25 Ari	24 Ari	23 Tau	25 Can	24 Leo	24 Vir	24 Sco	25 Cap	24 Aqu	25 Ari	25 Tau
26 Pis	27 Tau	27 Tau	25 Gem	28 Leo	26 Vir	26 Lib	26 Sag	27 Aqu	26 Pis	27 Tau	27 Gem
29 Ari		29 Gem	28 Can	30 Vir	29 Lib	28 Sco	28 Cap	29 Pis	29 Ari	30 Gem	30 Can
31 Tau			30 Leo			30 Sag	31 Aqu		31 Tau		

1907

JAN.	FEB.	MAR.	APR.	MAY	JUN.	JUL.	AUG.	SEP.	OCT.	NOV.	DEC.
1 Leo	2 Lib	1 Lib	2 Sag	1 Cap	2 Pis	1 Ari	2 Gem	1 Can	1 Leo	2 Lib	2 Sco
4 Vir	4 Sco	4 Sco	4 Cap	3 Aqu	4 Ari	4 Tau	5 Can	4 Leo	4 Vir	5 Sco	4 Sag
6 Lib	7 Sag	6 Sag	6 Aqu	6 Pis	6 Tau	6 Gem	7 Leo	6 Vir	6 Lib	7 Sag	6 Cap
8 Sco	9 Cap	8 Cap	8 Pis	8 Ari	9 Gem	9 Can	10 Vir	9 Lib	8 Sco	9 Cap	8 Aqu
10 Sag	11 Aqu	10 Aqu	11 Ari	10 Tau	11 Can	11 Leo	12 Lib	11 Sco	10 Sag	11 Aqu	10 Pis
12 Cap	13 Pis	12 Pis	13 Tau	13 Gem	14 Leo	14 Vir	15 Sco	13 Sag	13 Cap	13 Pis	12 Ari
14 Aqu	15 Ari	14 Ari	15 Gem	15 Can	16 Vir	16 Lib	17 Sag	15 Cap	15 Aqu	15 Ari	15 Tau
16 Pis	17 Tau	17 Tau	18 Can	18 Leo	19 Lib	18 Sco	19 Cap	17 Aqu	17 Pis	17 Tau	17 Gem
18 Ari	20 Gem	19 Gem	20 Leo	20 Vir	21 Sco	21 Sag	21 Aqu	19 Pis	19 Ari	20 Gem	20 Can
21 Tau	22 Can	22 Can	23 Vir	23 Lib	23 Sag	23 Cap	23 Pis	22 Ari	21 Tau	22 Can	22 Leo
23 Gem	25 Leo	24 Leo	25 Lib	25 Sco	25 Cap	25 Aqu	25 Ari	24 Tau	23 Gem	25 Leo	25 Vir
26 Can	27 Vir	27 Vir	27 Sco	27 Sag	27 Aqu	27 Pis	27 Tau	26 Gem	26 Can	27 Vir	27 Lib
28 Leo		29 Lib	29 Sag	29 Cap	29 Pis	29 Ari	30 Gem	29 Can	28 Leo	30 Lib	29 Sco
31 Vir		31 Sco		31 Aqu		31 Tau			31 Vir		

1908

JAN.	FEB.	MAR.	APR.	MAY	JUN.	JUL.	AUG.	SEP.	OCT.	NOV.	DEC.
1 Sag	1 Aqu	2 Pis	2 Tau	2 Gem	3 Leo	3 Vir	1 Lib	3 Sag	2 Cap	3 Pis	2 Ari
3 Cap	3 Pis	4 Ari	4 Gem	4 Can	5 Vir	5 Lib	4 Sco	5 Cap	4 Aqu	5 Ari	4 Tau
5 Aqu	5 Ari	6 Tau	7 Can	7 Leo	8 Lib	8 Sco	6 Sag	7 Aqu	6 Pis	7 Tau	6 Gem
7 Pis	7 Tau	8 Gem	9 Leo	9 Vir	10 Sco	10 Sag	8 Cap	9 Pis	8 Ari	9 Gem	9 Can
9 Ari	10 Gem	10 Can	12 Vir	11 Lib	12 Sag	12 Cap	10 Aqu	11 Ari	10 Tau	11 Can	11 Leo
11 Tau	12 Can	13 Leo	14 Lib	14 Sco	15 Cap	14 Aqu	12 Pis	13 Tau	12 Gem	14 Leo	13 Vir
13 Gem	15 Leo	15 Vir	16 Sco	16 Sag	17 Aqu	16 Pis	14 Ari	15 Gem	15 Can	16 Vir	16 Lib
16 Can	17 Vir	18 Lib	19 Sag	18 Cap	19 Pis	18 Ari	16 Tau	17 Can	17 Leo	19 Lib	18 Sco
18 Leo	20 Lib	20 Sco	21 Cap	20 Aqu	21 Ari	20 Tau	19 Gem	20 Leo	20 Vir	21 Sco	21 Sag
21 Vir	22 Sco	22 Sag	23 Aqu	22 Pis	23 Tau	22 Gem	21 Can	22 Vir	22 Lib	23 Sag	23 Cap
23 Lib	24 Sag	25 Cap	25 Pis	25 Ari	25 Gem	25 Can	24 Leo	25 Lib	25 Sco	26 Cap	25 Aqu
26 Sco	26 Cap	27 Aqu	27 Ari	27 Tau	28 Can	27 Leo	26 Vir	27 Sco	27 Sag	28 Aqu	27 Pis
28 Sag	29 Aqu	29 Pis	29 Tau	29 Gem	30 Leo	30 Vir	29 Lib	30 Sag	29 Cap	30 Pis	29 Ari
30 Cap		31 Ari		31 Can			31 Sco		31 Aqu		31 Tau

1909

JAN.	FEB.	MAR.	APR.	MAY	JUN.	JUL.	AUG.	SEP.	OCT.	NOV.	DEC.
3 Gem	1 Can	3 Leo	2 Vir	1 Lib	3 Sag	2 Cap	1 Aqu	1 Ari	1 Tau	1 Can	1 Leo
5 Can	4 Leo	5 Vir	4 Lib	4 Sco	5 Cap	4 Aqu	3 Pis	3 Tau	3 Gem	3 Leo	3 Vir
7 Leo	6 Vir	8 Lib	7 Sco	6 Sag	7 Aqu	6 Pis	5 Ari	5 Gem	5 Can	6 Vir	6 Lib
10 Vir	9 Lib	10 Sco	9 Sag	9 Cap	9 Pis	9 Ari	7 Tau	8 Can	7 Leo	8 Lib	8 Sco
12 Lib	11 Sco	13 Sag	11 Cap	11 Aqu	11 Ari	11 Tau	9 Gem	10 Leo	10 Vir	11 Sco	11 Sag
15 Sco	13 Sag	15 Cap	14 Aqu	13 Pis	13 Tau	13 Gem	11 Can	12 Vir	12 Lib	13 Sag	13 Cap
17 Sag	16 Cap	17 Aqu	16 Pis	15 Ari	16 Gem	15 Can	14 Leo	15 Lib	15 Sco	16 Cap	15 Aqu
19 Cap	18 Aqu	19 Pis	18 Ari	17 Tau	18 Can	17 Leo	16 Vir	17 Sco	17 Sag	18 Aqu	18 Pis
21 Aqu	20 Pis	21 Ari	20 Tau	19 Gem	20 Leo	20 Vir	19 Lib	20 Sag	20 Cap	20 Pis	20 Ari
23 Pis	22 Ari	23 Tau	22 Gem	21 Can	22 Vir	22 Lib	21 Sco	22 Cap	22 Aqu	23 Ari	22 Tau
25 Ari	24 Tau	25 Gem	24 Can	24 Leo	25 Lib	25 Sco	24 Sag	25 Aqu	24 Pis	25 Tau	24 Gem
28 Tau	26 Gem	28 Can	26 Leo	26 Vir	27 Sco	27 Sag	26 Cap	27 Pis	26 Ari	27 Gem	26 Can
30 Gem	28 Can	30 Leo	29 Vir	29 Lib	30 Sag	30 Cap	28 Aqu	29 Ari	28 Tau	29 Can	28 Leo
				31 Sco			30 Pis		30 Gem		31 Vir

1910

JAN.	FEB.	MAR.	APR.	MAY	JUN.	JUL.	AUG.	SEP.	OCT.	NOV.	DEC.
2 Lib	1 Sco	3 Sag	2 Cap	1 Aqu	2 Ari	1 Tau	2 Can	2 Vir	2 Lib	1 Sco	1 Sag
5 Sco	3 Sag	5 Cap	4 Aqu	3 Pis	4 Tau	3 Gem	4 Leo	5 Lib	5 Sco	3 Sag	3 Cap
7 Sag	6 Cap	8 Aqu	6 Pis	6 Ari	6 Gem	5 Can	6 Vir	7 Sco	7 Sag	6 Cap	6 Aqu
9 Cap	8 Aqu	10 Pis	8 Ari	8 Tau	8 Can	8 Leo	8 Lib	10 Sag	10 Cap	8 Aqu	8 Pis
12 Aqu	10 Pis	12 Ari	10 Tau	10 Gem	10 Leo	10 Vir	11 Sco	12 Cap	12 Aqu	11 Pis	10 Ari
14 Pis	12 Ari	14 Tau	12 Gem	12 Can	12 Vir	12 Lib	13 Sag	15 Aqu	14 Pis	13 Ari	12 Tau
16 Ari	14 Tau	16 Gem	14 Can	14 Leo	15 Lib	15 Sco	16 Cap	17 Pis	16 Ari	15 Tau	14 Gem
18 Tau	16 Gem	18 Can	16 Leo	16 Vir	17 Sco	17 Sag	18 Aqu	19 Ari	18 Tau	17 Gem	16 Can
20 Gem	19 Can	20 Leo	19 Vir	18 Lib	20 Sag	20 Cap	21 Pis	21 Tau	20 Gem	19 Can	18 Leo
22 Can	21 Leo	23 Vir	21 Lib	21 Sco	22 Cap	22 Aqu	23 Ari	23 Gem	23 Can	21 Leo	21 Vir
25 Leo	23 Vir	25 Lib	24 Sco	24 Sag	25 Aqu	24 Pis	25 Tau	25 Can	25 Leo	23 Vir	23 Lib
27 Vir	26 Lib	28 Sco	26 Sag	26 Cap	27 Pis	26 Ari	27 Gem	27 Leo	27 Vir	26 Lib	25 Sco
29 Lib	28 Sco	30 Sag	29 Cap	28 Aqu	29 Ari	29 Tau	29 Can	30 Vir	29 Lib	28 Sco	28 Sag
				31 Pis		31 Gem	31 Leo				30 Cap

1911

JAN.	FEB.	MAR.	APR.	MAY	JUN.	JUL.	AUG.	SEP.	OCT.	NOV.	DEC.
2 Aqu	3 Ari	2 Ari	1 Tau	2 Can	3 Vir	2 Lib	1 Sco	2 Cap	2 Aqu	1 Pis	3 Tau
4 Pis	5 Tau	4 Tau	3 Gem	4 Leo	5 Lib	4 Sco	3 Sag	5 Aqu	4 Pis	3 Ari	5 Gem
6 Ari	7 Gem	6 Gem	5 Can	6 Vir	7 Sco	7 Sag	6 Cap	7 Pis	7 Ari	5 Tau	7 Can
9 Tau	9 Can	8 Can	7 Leo	9 Lib	10 Sag	10 Cap	8 Aqu	9 Ari	9 Tau	7 Gem	9 Leo
11 Gem	11 Leo	11 Leo	9 Vir	11 Sco	12 Cap	12 Aqu	11 Pis	12 Tau	11 Gem	9 Can	11 Vir
13 Can	13 Vir	13 Vir	11 Lib	13 Sag	15 Aqu	14 Pis	13 Ari	14 Gem	13 Can	11 Leo	13 Lib
15 Leo	16 Lib	15 Lib	14 Sco	16 Cap	17 Pis	17 Ari	15 Tau	16 Can	15 Leo	14 Vir	15 Sco
17 Vir	18 Sco	17 Sco	16 Sag	19 Aqu	20 Ari	19 Tau	17 Gem	18 Leo	17 Vir	16 Lib	18 Sag
19 Lib	21 Sag	20 Sag	19 Cap	21 Pis	22 Tau	21 Gem	20 Can	20 Vir	20 Lib	18 Sco	20 Cap
22 Sco	23 Cap	22 Cap	21 Aqu	23 Ari	24 Gem	23 Can	22 Leo	22 Lib	22 Sco	21 Sag	23 Aqu
24 Sag	26 Aqu	25 Aqu	24 Pis	25 Tau	26 Can	25 Leo	24 Vir	25 Sco	24 Sag	23 Cap	25 Pis
27 Cap	28 Pis	27 Pis	26 Ari	27 Gem	28 Leo	27 Vir	26 Lib	27 Sag	27 Cap	26 Aqu	28 Ari
29 Aqu		29 Ari	28 Tau	29 Can	30 Vir	29 Lib	28 Sco	29 Cap	29 Aqu	28 Pis	30 Tau
31 Pis			30 Gem	31 Leo			31 Sag			30 Ari	

1912

JAN.	FEB.	MAR.	APR.	MAY	JUN.	JUL.	AUG.	SEP.	OCT.	NOV.	DEC.
1 Gem	2 Leo	2 Vir	1 Lib	2 Sag	1 Cap	1 Aqu	2 Ari	1 Tau	3 Can	1 Leo	2 Lib
3 Can	4 Vir	4 Lib	3 Sco	5 Cap	4 Aqu	3 Pis	5 Tau	3 Gem	5 Leo	3 Vir	5 Sco
5 Leo	6 Lib	6 Sco	5 Sag	7 Aqu	6 Pis	6 Ari	7 Gem	5 Can	7 Vir	5 Lib	7 Sag
7 Vir	8 Sco	9 Sag	8 Cap	10 Pis	9 Ari	8 Tau	9 Can	7 Leo	9 Lib	7 Sco	9 Cap
9 Lib	10 Sag	11 Cap	10 Aqu	12 Ari	11 Tau	11 Gem	11 Leo	9 Vir	11 Sco	10 Sag	12 Aqu
12 Sco	13 Cap	14 Aqu	13 Pis	15 Tau	13 Gem	13 Can	13 Vir	11 Lib	13 Sag	12 Cap	14 Pis
14 Sag	15 Aqu	16 Pis	15 Ari	17 Gem	15 Can	15 Leo	15 Lib	14 Sco	16 Cap	14 Aqu	17 Ari
17 Cap	18 Pis	19 Ari	17 Tau	19 Can	17 Leo	17 Vir	17 Sco	16 Sag	18 Aqu	17 Pis	19 Tau
19 Aqu	20 Ari	21 Tau	19 Gem	21 Leo	19 Vir	19 Lib	19 Sag	18 Cap	21 Pis	19 Ari	21 Gem
22 Pis	23 Tau	23 Gem	21 Can	23 Vir	21 Lib	21 Sco	22 Cap	21 Aqu	23 Ari	22 Tau	24 Can
24 Ari	25 Gem	25 Can	24 Leo	25 Lib	24 Sco	23 Sag	24 Aqu	23 Pis	25 Tau	24 Gem	26 Leo
26 Tau	27 Can	27 Leo	26 Vir	27 Sco	26 Sag	26 Cap	27 Pis	26 Ari	28 Gem	26 Can	28 Vir
29 Gem	29 Leo	29 Vir	28 Lib	30 Sag	28 Cap	28 Aqu	29 Ari	28 Tau	30 Can	28 Leo	30 Lib
31 Can			30 Sco			31 Pis		30 Gem		30 Vir	

1913

JAN.	FEB.	MAR.	APR.	MAY	JUN.	JUL.	AUG.	SEP.	OCT.	NOV.	DEC.
1 Sco	2 Cap	1 Cap	2 Pis	2 Ari	1 Tau	1 Gem	1 Leo	2 Lib	1 Sco	2 Cap	2 Aqu
3 Sag	4 Aqu	4 Aqu	5 Ari	5 Tau	3 Gem	3 Can	3 Vir	4 Sco	3 Sag	4 Aqu	4 Pis
6 Cap	7 Pis	6 Pis	7 Tau	7 Gem	6 Can	5 Leo	5 Lib	6 Sag	6 Cap	7 Pis	7 Ari
8 Aqu	9 Ari	9 Ari	10 Gem	9 Can	8 Leo	7 Vir	8 Sco	8 Cap	8 Aqu	9 Ari	9 Tau
11 Pis	12 Tau	11 Tau	12 Can	11 Leo	10 Vir	9 Lib	10 Sag	11 Aqu	10 Pis	12 Tau	12 Gem
13 Ari	14 Gem	13 Gem	14 Leo	14 Vir	12 Lib	11 Sco	12 Cap	13 Pis	13 Ari	14 Gem	14 Can
16 Tau	16 Can	16 Can	16 Vir	16 Lib	14 Sco	13 Sag	14 Aqu	16 Ari	15 Tau	17 Can	16 Leo
18 Gem	18 Leo	18 Leo	18 Lib	18 Sco	16 Sag	16 Cap	17 Pis	18 Tau	18 Gem	19 Leo	18 Vir
20 Can	20 Vir	20 Vir	20 Sco	20 Sag	18 Cap	18 Aqu	19 Ari	21 Gem	20 Can	21 Vir	20 Lib
22 Leo	22 Lib	22 Lib	23 Sag	22 Cap	21 Aqu	21 Pis	22 Tau	23 Can	23 Leo	23 Lib	22 Sco
24 Vir	25 Sco	24 Sco	25 Cap	24 Aqu	23 Pis	23 Ari	24 Gem	25 Leo	25 Vir	25 Sco	25 Sag
26 Lib	27 Sag	26 Sag	27 Aqu	27 Pis	26 Ari	26 Tau	27 Can	27 Vir	27 Lib	27 Sag	27 Cap
28 Sco		28 Cap	30 Pis	30 Ari	28 Tau	28 Gem	29 Leo	29 Lib	29 Sco	29 Cap	29 Aqu
30 Sag		31 Aqu				30 Can	31 Vir		31 Sag		31 Pis

1914

JAN.	FEB.	MAR.	APR.	MAY	JUN.	JUL.	AUG.	SEP.	OCT.	NOV.	DEC.
3 Ari	2 Tau	1 Tau	2 Can	2 Leo	2 Lib	2 Sco	2 Cap	1 Aqu	3 Ari	2 Tau	1 Gem
5 Tau	4 Gem	4 Gem	5 Leo	4 Vir	5 Sco	4 Sag	5 Aqu	3 Pis	5 Tau	4 Gem	4 Can
8 Gem	7 Can	6 Can	7 Vir	6 Lib	7 Sag	6 Cap	7 Pis	6 Ari	8 Gem	7 Can	6 Leo
10 Can	9 Leo	8 Leo	9 Lib	8 Sco	9 Cap	8 Aqu	9 Ari	8 Tau	10 Can	9 Leo	9 Vir
12 Leo	11 Vir	10 Vir	11 Sco	10 Sag	11 Aqu	11 Pis	12 Tau	11 Gem	13 Leo	11 Vir	11 Lib
14 Vir	13 Lib	12 Lib	13 Sag	12 Cap	13 Pis	13 Ari	14 Gem	13 Can	15 Vir	14 Lib	13 Sco
17 Lib	15 Sco	14 Sco	15 Cap	14 Aqu	16 Ari	15 Tau	17 Can	15 Leo	17 Lib	16 Sco	15 Sag
19 Sco	17 Sag	16 Sag	17 Aqu	17 Pis	18 Tau	18 Gem	19 Leo	18 Vir	19 Sco	18 Sag	17 Cap
21 Sag	19 Cap	19 Cap	20 Pis	19 Ari	21 Gem	20 Can	21 Vir	20 Lib	21 Sag	20 Cap	19 Aqu
23 Cap	22 Aqu	21 Aqu	22 Ari	22 Tau	23 Can	23 Leo	23 Lib	22 Sco	23 Cap	22 Aqu	21 Pis
25 Aqu	24 Pis	23 Pis	25 Tau	24 Gem	25 Leo	25 Vir	25 Sco	24 Sag	25 Aqu	24 Pis	24 Ari
28 Pis	27 Ari	26 Ari	27 Gem	27 Can	28 Vir	27 Lib	27 Sag	26 Cap	28 Pis	26 Ari	26 Tau
30 Ari		28 Tau	30 Can	29 Leo	30 Lib	29 Sco	30 Cap	28 Aqu	30 Ari	29 Tau	29 Gem
		31 Gem		31 Vir		31 Sag		30 Pis			31 Can

1915

JAN.	FEB.	MAR.	APR.	MAY	JUN.	JUL.	AUG.	SEP.	OCT.	NOV.	DEC.
3 Leo	1 Vir	1 Vir	1 Sco	1 Sag	1 Aqu	1 Pis	2 Tau	3 Can	3 Leo	2 Vir	1 Lib
5 Vir	3 Lib	3 Lib	3 Sag	3 Cap	3 Pis	3 Ari	4 Gem	5 Leo	5 Vir	4 Lib	3 Sco
7 Lib	5 Sco	5 Sco	5 Cap	5 Aqu	6 Ari	5 Tau	7 Can	8 Vir	7 Lib	6 Sco	5 Sag
9 Sco	8 Sag	7 Sag	7 Aqu	7 Pis	8 Tau	8 Gem	9 Leo	10 Lib	9 Sco	8 Sag	7 Cap
11 Sag	10 Cap	9 Cap	10 Pis	9 Ari	11 Gem	10 Can	11 Vir	12 Sco	12 Sag	10 Cap	9 Aqu
13 Cap	12 Aqu	11 Aqu	12 Ari	12 Tau	13 Can	13 Leo	14 Lib	14 Sag	14 Cap	12 Aqu	11 Pis
16 Aqu	14 Pis	13 Pis	15 Tau	14 Gem	16 Leo	15 Vir	16 Sco	16 Cap	16 Aqu	14 Pis	14 Ari
18 Pis	16 Ari	16 Ari	17 Gem	17 Can	18 Vir	17 Lib	18 Sag	18 Aqu	18 Pis	16 Ari	16 Tau
20 Ari	19 Tau	18 Tau	20 Can	19 Leo	20 Lib	20 Sco	20 Cap	21 Pis	20 Ari	19 Tau	19 Gem
23 Tau	21 Gem	21 Gem	22 Leo	22 Vir	22 Sco	22 Sag	22 Aqu	23 Ari	23 Tau	21 Gem	21 Can
25 Gem	24 Can	23 Can	24 Vir	24 Lib	24 Sag	24 Cap	24 Pis	25 Tau	25 Gem	24 Can	24 Leo
28 Can	26 Leo	26 Leo	27 Lib	26 Sco	26 Cap	26 Aqu	27 Ari	28 Gem	28 Can	26 Leo	26 Vir
30 Leo		28 Vir	29 Sco	28 Sag	28 Aqu	28 Pis	29 Tau	30 Can	30 Leo	29 Vir	29 Lib
		30 Lib		30 Cap		30 Ari	30 Gem				31 Sco

45

1916

JAN.	FEB.	MAR.	APR.	MAY	JUN.	JUL.	AUG.	SEP.	OCT.	NOV.	DEC.
2 Sag	2 Aqu	1 Aqu	1 Ari	1 Tau	2 Can	2 Leo	1 Vir	2 Sco	1 Sag	2 Aqu	1 Pis
4 Cap	4 Pis	3 Pis	4 Tau	3 Gem	5 Leo	4 Vir	3 Lib	4 Sag	3 Cap	4 Pis	3 Ari
6 Aqu	6 Ari	5 Ari	6 Gem	6 Can	7 Vir	7 Lib	5 Sco	6 Cap	5 Aqu	6 Ari	5 Tau
8 Pis	9 Tau	7 Tau	8 Can	8 Leo	9 Lib	9 Sco	8 Sag	8 Aqu	7 Pis	8 Tau	8 Gem
10 Ari	11 Gem	10 Gem	11 Leo	11 Vir	12 Sco	11 Sag	10 Cap	10 Pis	10 Ari	10 Gem	10 Can
12 Tau	14 Can	12 Can	13 Vir	13 Lib	14 Sag	13 Cap	12 Aqu	12 Ari	12 Tau	13 Can	13 Leo
15 Gem	16 Leo	15 Leo	16 Lib	15 Sco	16 Cap	15 Aqu	14 Pis	14 Tau	14 Gem	15 Leo	15 Vir
17 Can	19 Vir	17 Vir	18 Sco	17 Sag	18 Aqu	17 Pis	16 Ari	17 Gem	16 Can	18 Vir	18 Lib
20 Leo	21 Lib	19 Lib	20 Sag	19 Cap	20 Pis	19 Ari	18 Tau	19 Can	19 Leo	20 Lib	20 Sco
22 Vir	23 Sco	22 Sco	22 Cap	21 Aqu	22 Ari	22 Tau	20 Gem	22 Leo	21 Vir	23 Sco	22 Sag
25 Lib	25 Sag	24 Sag	24 Aqu	24 Pis	24 Tau	24 Gem	23 Can	24 Vir	24 Lib	25 Sag	24 Cap
27 Sco	28 Cap	26 Cap	26 Pis	26 Ari	27 Gem	26 Can	25 Leo	27 Lib	26 Sco	27 Cap	26 Aqu
29 Sag		28 Aqu	29 Ari	28 Tau	29 Can	29 Leo	28 Vir	29 Sco	28 Sag	29 Aqu	28 Pis
31 Cap		30 Pis		30 Gem			30 Lib		30 Cap		30 Ari

1917

JAN.	FEB.	MAR.	APR.	MAY	JUN.	JUL.	AUG.	SEP.	OCT.	NOV.	DEC.
2 Tau	3 Can	2 Can	1 Leo	1 Vir	2 Sco	1 Sag	2 Aqu	2 Ari	2 Tau	3 Can	2 Leo
4 Gem	5 Leo	4 Leo	3 Vir	3 Lib	4 Sag	4 Cap	4 Pis	4 Tau	4 Gem	5 Leo	5 Vir
6 Can	8 Vir	7 Vir	6 Lib	5 Sco	6 Cap	6 Aqu	6 Ari	7 Gem	6 Can	8 Vir	7 Lib
9 Leo	10 Lib	9 Lib	8 Sco	8 Sag	8 Aqu	8 Pis	8 Tau	9 Can	9 Leo	10 Lib	10 Sco
11 Vir	13 Sco	12 Sco	10 Sag	10 Cap	10 Pis	10 Ari	10 Gem	11 Leo	11 Vir	13 Sco	12 Sag
14 Lib	15 Sag	14 Sag	13 Cap	12 Aqu	12 Ari	12 Tau	13 Can	14 Vir	14 Lib	15 Sag	14 Cap
16 Sco	17 Cap	16 Cap	15 Aqu	14 Pis	15 Tau	14 Gem	15 Leo	17 Lib	16 Sco	17 Cap	17 Aqu
19 Sag	19 Aqu	18 Aqu	17 Pis	16 Ari	17 Gem	16 Can	18 Vir	19 Sco	19 Sag	19 Aqu	19 Pis
21 Cap	21 Pis	21 Pis	19 Ari	18 Tau	19 Can	19 Leo	20 Lib	21 Sag	21 Cap	22 Pis	21 Ari
23 Aqu	23 Ari	23 Ari	21 Tau	21 Gem	22 Leo	21 Vir	23 Sco	24 Cap	23 Aqu	24 Ari	23 Tau
25 Pis	25 Tau	25 Tau	23 Gem	23 Can	24 Vir	24 Lib	25 Sag	26 Aqu	25 Pis	26 Tau	25 Gem
27 Ari	27 Gem	27 Gem	26 Can	25 Leo	27 Lib	26 Sco	27 Cap	28 Pis	27 Ari	28 Gem	27 Can
29 Tau		29 Can	28 Leo	28 Vir	29 Sco	29 Sag	29 Aqu	30 Ari	29 Tau	30 Can	30 Leo
31 Gem				30 Lib		31 Cap	31 Pis		31 Gem		

1918

JAN.	FEB.	MAR.	APR.	MAY	JUN.	JUL.	AUG.	SEP.	OCT.	NOV.	DEC.
1 Vir	3 Sco	2 Sco	1 Sag	3 Aqu	1 Pis	2 Tau	1 Gem	2 Leo	1 Vir	2 Sco	2 Sag
4 Lib	5 Sag	4 Sag	3 Cap	5 Pis	3 Ari	5 Gem	3 Can	4 Vir	4 Lib	5 Sag	5 Cap
6 Sco	7 Cap	7 Cap	5 Aqu	7 Ari	5 Tau	7 Can	5 Leo	6 Lib	6 Sco	7 Cap	7 Aqu
9 Sag	9 Aqu	9 Aqu	7 Pis	9 Tau	7 Gem	9 Leo	8 Vir	9 Sco	9 Sag	10 Aqu	9 Pis
11 Cap	11 Pis	11 Pis	9 Ari	11 Gem	9 Can	11 Vir	10 Lib	11 Sag	11 Cap	12 Pis	11 Ari
13 Aqu	13 Ari	13 Ari	11 Tau	13 Can	12 Leo	14 Lib	13 Sco	14 Cap	14 Aqu	14 Ari	14 Tau
15 Pis	15 Tau	15 Tau	13 Gem	15 Leo	14 Vir	16 Sco	15 Sag	16 Aqu	16 Pis	16 Tau	16 Gem
17 Ari	18 Gem	17 Gem	16 Can	18 Vir	17 Lib	19 Sag	18 Cap	18 Pis	18 Ari	18 Gem	18 Can
19 Tau	20 Can	19 Can	18 Leo	20 Lib	19 Sco	21 Cap	20 Aqu	20 Ari	20 Tau	20 Can	20 Leo
21 Gem	22 Leo	22 Leo	20 Vir	23 Sco	21 Sag	23 Aqu	22 Pis	22 Tau	22 Gem	22 Leo	22 Vir
24 Can	25 Vir	24 Vir	23 Lib	25 Sag	24 Cap	25 Pis	24 Ari	24 Gem	24 Can	25 Vir	25 Lib
26 Leo	27 Lib	27 Lib	25 Sco	27 Cap	26 Aqu	27 Ari	26 Tau	26 Can	26 Leo	27 Lib	27 Sco
29 Vir		29 Sco	28 Sag	30 Aqu	28 Pis	30 Tau	28 Gem	29 Leo	28 Vir	30 Sco	30 Sag
31 Lib			30 Cap		30 Ari		30 Can		31 Lib		

1919

JAN.	FEB.	MAR.	APR.	MAY	JUN.	JUL.	AUG.	SEP.	OCT.	NOV.	DEC.
1 Cap	2 Pis	1 Pis	2 Tau	1 Gem	2 Leo	1 Vir	2 Sco	1 Sag	1 Cap	2 Pis	2 Ari
3 Aqu	4 Ari	3 Ari	4 Gem	3 Can	4 Vir	4 Lib	5 Sag	4 Cap	4 Aqu	4 Ari	4 Tau
6 Pis	6 Tau	5 Tau	6 Can	5 Leo	6 Lib	6 Sco	7 Cap	6 Aqu	6 Pis	7 Tau	6 Gem
8 Ari	8 Gem	7 Gem	8 Leo	8 Vir	9 Sco	9 Sag	10 Aqu	8 Pis	8 Ari	9 Gem	8 Can
10 Tau	10 Can	10 Can	10 Vir	10 Lib	11 Sag	11 Cap	12 Pis	11 Ari	10 Tau	11 Can	10 Leo
12 Gem	13 Leo	12 Leo	13 Lib	13 Sco	14 Cap	14 Aqu	14 Ari	13 Tau	12 Gem	13 Leo	12 Vir
14 Can	15 Vir	14 Vir	15 Sco	15 Sag	16 Aqu	16 Pis	16 Tau	15 Gem	14 Can	15 Vir	14 Lib
16 Leo	17 Lib	17 Lib	18 Sag	18 Cap	19 Pis	18 Ari	19 Gem	17 Can	16 Leo	17 Lib	17 Sco
18 Vir	20 Sco	19 Sco	20 Cap	20 Aqu	21 Ari	20 Tau	21 Can	19 Leo	19 Vir	20 Sco	19 Sag
21 Lib	22 Sag	22 Sag	23 Aqu	23 Pis	23 Tau	22 Gem	23 Leo	21 Vir	21 Lib	22 Sag	22 Cap
23 Sco	25 Cap	24 Cap	25 Pis	25 Ari	25 Gem	24 Can	25 Vir	24 Lib	23 Sco	25 Cap	24 Aqu
26 Sag	27 Aqu	26 Aqu	27 Ari	27 Tau	27 Can	27 Leo	27 Lib	26 Sco	26 Sag	27 Aqu	27 Pis
28 Cap		29 Pis	29 Tau	29 Gem	29 Leo	29 Vir	30 Sco	29 Sag	28 Cap	30 Pis	29 Ari
31 Aqu		31 Ari		31 Can		31 Lib			31 Aqu		31 Tau

1920

JAN.	FEB.	MAR.	APR.	MAY	JUN.	JUL.	AUG.	SEP.	OCT.	NOV.	DEC.
2 Gem	1 Can	1 Leo	2 Lib	2 Sco	3 Cap	3 Aqu	1 Pis	2 Tau	2 Gem	2 Leo	1 Vir
4 Can	3 Leo	3 Vir	4 Sco	4 Sag	5 Aqu	5 Pis	4 Ari	4 Gem	4 Can	4 Vir	4 Lib
6 Leo	5 Vir	6 Lib	7 Sag	7 Cap	8 Pis	7 Ari	6 Tau	7 Can	6 Leo	6 Lib	6 Sco
9 Vir	7 Lib	8 Sco	9 Cap	9 Aqu	10 Ari	10 Tau	8 Gem	9 Leo	8 Vir	9 Sco	8 Sag
11 Lib	10 Sco	10 Sag	12 Aqu	12 Pis	12 Tau	12 Gem	10 Can	11 Vir	10 Lib	11 Sag	11 Cap
13 Sco	12 Sag	13 Cap	14 Pis	14 Ari	14 Gem	14 Can	12 Leo	13 Lib	12 Sco	14 Cap	13 Aqu
16 Sag	15 Cap	15 Aqu	16 Ari	16 Tau	16 Can	16 Leo	14 Vir	15 Sco	15 Sag	16 Aqu	16 Pis
18 Cap	17 Aqu	18 Pis	19 Tau	18 Gem	18 Leo	18 Vir	16 Lib	17 Sag	17 Cap	19 Pis	18 Ari
21 Aqu	19 Pis	20 Ari	21 Gem	20 Can	20 Vir	20 Lib	19 Sco	20 Cap	20 Aqu	21 Ari	21 Tau
23 Pis	22 Ari	22 Tau	23 Can	22 Leo	23 Lib	22 Sco	21 Sag	22 Aqu	22 Pis	23 Tau	23 Gem
25 Ari	24 Tau	24 Gem	25 Leo	24 Vir	25 Sco	25 Sag	24 Cap	25 Pis	25 Ari	25 Gem	25 Can
28 Tau	26 Gem	26 Can	27 Vir	26 Lib	28 Sag	27 Cap	26 Aqu	27 Ari	27 Tau	27 Can	27 Leo
30 Gem	28 Can	28 Leo	29 Lib	29 Sco	30 Cap	30 Aqu	29 Pis	29 Tau	29 Gem	29 Leo	29 Vir
		31 Vir		31 Sag			31 Ari		31 Can		31 Lib

1921

JAN.	FEB.	MAR.	APR.	MAY	JUN.	JUL.	AUG.	SEP.	OCT.	NOV.	DEC.
2 Sco	1 Sag	3 Cap	2 Aqu	1 Pis	3 Tau	2 Gem	1 Can	1 Vir	3 Sco	1 Sag	1 Cap
5 Sag	3 Cap	5 Aqu	4 Pis	4 Ari	5 Gem	4 Can	3 Leo	3 Lib	5 Sag	3 Cap	3 Aqu
7 Cap	6 Aqu	8 Pis	6 Ari	6 Tau	7 Can	6 Leo	5 Vir	5 Sco	7 Cap	6 Aqu	6 Pis
10 Aqu	8 Pis	10 Ari	9 Tau	8 Gem	9 Leo	8 Vir	7 Lib	7 Sag	10 Aqu	8 Pis	8 Ari
12 Pis	11 Ari	13 Tau	11 Gem	10 Can	11 Vir	10 Lib	9 Sco	10 Cap	12 Pis	11 Ari	11 Tau
15 Ari	13 Tau	15 Gem	13 Can	13 Leo	13 Lib	12 Sco	11 Sag	12 Aqu	15 Ari	13 Tau	13 Gem
17 Tau	16 Gem	17 Can	15 Leo	15 Vir	15 Sco	15 Sag	14 Cap	15 Pis	17 Tau	16 Gem	15 Can
19 Gem	18 Can	19 Leo	17 Vir	17 Lib	18 Sag	17 Cap	16 Aqu	17 Ari	19 Gem	18 Can	17 Leo
21 Can	20 Leo	21 Vir	20 Lib	19 Sco	20 Cap	20 Aqu	19 Pis	20 Tau	22 Can	20 Leo	19 Vir
23 Leo	22 Vir	23 Lib	22 Sco	21 Sag	23 Aqu	22 Pis	21 Ari	22 Gem	24 Leo	22 Vir	22 Lib
25 Vir	24 Lib	25 Sco	24 Sag	24 Cap	25 Pis	25 Ari	24 Tau	24 Can	26 Vir	24 Lib	24 Sco
27 Lib	26 Sco	28 Sag	26 Cap	26 Aqu	28 Ari	27 Tau	26 Gem	26 Leo	28 Lib	26 Sco	26 Sag
30 Sco	28 Sag	30 Cap	29 Aqu	29 Pis	30 Tau	30 Gem	28 Can	28 Vir	30 Sco	29 Sag	28 Cap
				31 Ari			30 Leo	30 Lib			31 Aqu

1922

JAN.	FEB.	MAR.	APR.	MAY	JUN.	JUL.	AUG.	SEP.	OCT.	NOV.	DEC.
2 Pis	1 Ari	3 Tau	1 Gem	1 Can	1 Vir	1 Lib	1 Sag	2 Aqu	2 Pis	1 Ari	1 Tau
5 Ari	3 Tau	5 Gem	4 Can	3 Leo	4 Lib	3 Sco	4 Cap	5 Pis	5 Ari	3 Tau	3 Gem
7 Tau	6 Gem	7 Can	6 Leo	5 Vir	6 Sco	5 Sag	6 Aqu	7 Ari	7 Tau	6 Gem	5 Can
9 Gem	8 Can	10 Leo	8 Vir	7 Lib	8 Sag	7 Cap	8 Pis	10 Tau	10 Gem	8 Can	8 Leo
12 Can	10 Leo	12 Vir	10 Lib	9 Sco	10 Cap	10 Aqu	11 Ari	12 Gem	12 Can	10 Leo	10 Vir
14 Leo	12 Vir	13 Lib	12 Sco	11 Sag	12 Aqu	12 Pis	14 Tau	15 Can	14 Leo	13 Vir	12 Lib
16 Vir	14 Lib	16 Sco	14 Sag	14 Cap	15 Pis	15 Ari	16 Gem	17 Leo	16 Vir	15 Lib	14 Sco
18 Lib	16 Sco	18 Sag	16 Cap	16 Aqu	17 Ari	17 Tau	18 Can	19 Vir	18 Lib	17 Sco	16 Sag
20 Sco	18 Sag	20 Cap	19 Aqu	19 Pis	20 Tau	20 Gem	20 Leo	21 Lib	20 Sco	19 Sag	18 Cap
22 Sag	21 Cap	22 Aqu	21 Pis	21 Ari	22 Gem	22 Can	22 Vir	23 Sco	22 Sag	21 Cap	21 Aqu
24 Cap	23 Aqu	25 Pis	24 Ari	24 Tau	24 Can	24 Leo	24 Lib	25 Sag	24 Cap	23 Aqu	23 Pis
27 Aqu	26 Pis	27 Ari	26 Tau	26 Gem	27 Leo	26 Vir	26 Sco	27 Cap	27 Aqu	26 Pis	25 Ari
29 Pis	28 Ari	30 Tau	28 Gem	28 Can	29 Vir	28 Lib	29 Sag	30 Aqu	29 Pis	28 Ari	28 Tau
				30 Leo		30 Sco	31 Cap				30 Gem

1923

JAN.	FEB.	MAR.	APR.	MAY	JUN.	JUL.	AUG.	SEP.	OCT.	NOV.	DEC.
2 Can	2 Vir	2 Vir	2 Sco	2 Sag	2 Aqu	2 Pis	1 Ari	2 Gem	2 Can	1 Leo	3 Lib
4 Leo	4 Lib	4 Lib	4 Sag	4 Cap	5 Pis	4 Ari	3 Tau	5 Can	4 Leo	3 Vir	5 Sco
6 Vir	7 Sco	6 Sco	6 Cap	6 Aqu	7 Ari	7 Tau	6 Gem	7 Leo	7 Vir	5 Lib	7 Sag
8 Lib	9 Sag	8 Sag	9 Aqu	8 Pis	10 Tau	10 Gem	8 Can	9 Vir	9 Lib	7 Sco	9 Cap
10 Sco	11 Cap	10 Cap	11 Pis	11 Ari	12 Gem	12 Can	11 Leo	11 Lib	11 Sco	9 Sag	11 Aqu
12 Sag	13 Aqu	12 Aqu	14 Ari	13 Tau	15 Can	14 Leo	13 Vir	13 Sco	13 Sag	11 Cap	13 Pis
15 Cap	16 Pis	15 Pis	16 Tau	16 Gem	17 Leo	16 Vir	15 Lib	15 Sag	15 Cap	13 Aqu	15 Ari
17 Aqu	18 Ari	17 Ari	19 Gem	18 Can	19 Vir	19 Lib	17 Sco	17 Cap	17 Aqu	16 Pis	18 Tau
19 Pis	21 Tau	20 Tau	21 Can	21 Leo	21 Lib	21 Sco	19 Sag	20 Aqu	19 Pis	18 Ari	20 Gem
22 Ari	23 Gem	22 Gem	23 Leo	23 Vir	24 Sco	23 Sag	21 Cap	22 Pis	22 Ari	20 Tau	23 Can
24 Tau	26 Can	25 Can	26 Vir	25 Lib	26 Sag	25 Cap	23 Aqu	24 Ari	24 Tau	23 Gem	25 Leo
27 Gem	28 Leo	27 Leo	28 Lib	27 Sco	28 Cap	27 Aqu	26 Pis	27 Tau	27 Gem	26 Can	28 Vir
29 Can		29 Vir	30 Sco	29 Sag	30 Aqu	29 Pis	28 Ari	30 Gem	29 Can	28 Leo	30 Lib
31 Leo		31 Lib		31 Cap			31 Tau			30 Vir	

1924

JAN.	FEB.	MAR.	APR.	MAY	JUN.	JUL.	AUG.	SEP.	OCT.	NOV.	DEC.
1 Sco	1 Cap	2 Aqu	3 Ari	2 Tau	1 Gem	1 Can	2 Vir	1 Lib	2 Sag	1 Cap	2 Pis
3 Sag	3 Aqu	4 Pis	5 Tau	5 Gem	4 Can	3 Leo	4 Lib	3 Sco	4 Cap	3 Aqu	4 Ari
5 Cap	6 Pis	6 Ari	8 Gem	7 Can	6 Leo	6 Vir	7 Sco	5 Sag	6 Aqu	5 Pis	7 Tau
7 Aqu	8 Ari	9 Tau	10 Can	10 Leo	9 Vir	8 Lib	9 Sag	7 Cap	9 Pis	7 Ari	9 Gem
9 Pis	10 Tau	11 Gem	13 Leo	12 Vir	11 Lib	10 Sco	11 Cap	9 Aqu	11 Ari	9 Tau	12 Can
12 Ari	13 Gem	14 Can	15 Vir	15 Lib	13 Sco	12 Sag	13 Aqu	11 Pis	13 Tau	12 Gem	14 Leo
14 Tau	15 Can	16 Leo	17 Lib	17 Sco	15 Sag	14 Cap	15 Pis	14 Ari	16 Gem	14 Can	17 Vir
17 Gem	18 Leo	19 Vir	19 Sco	19 Sag	17 Cap	16 Aqu	17 Ari	16 Tau	18 Can	17 Leo	19 Lib
19 Can	20 Vir	21 Lib	21 Sag	21 Cap	19 Aqu	19 Pis	19 Tau	18 Gem	21 Leo	19 Vir	21 Sco
21 Leo	22 Lib	23 Sco	23 Cap	23 Aqu	21 Pis	21 Ari	22 Gem	21 Can	23 Vir	22 Lib	23 Sag
24 Vir	24 Sco	25 Sag	25 Aqu	25 Pis	23 Ari	23 Tau	24 Can	23 Leo	25 Lib	24 Sco	25 Cap
26 Lib	27 Sag	27 Cap	28 Pis	27 Ari	26 Tau	26 Gem	27 Leo	26 Vir	27 Sco	26 Sag	27 Aqu
28 Sco	29 Cap	29 Aqu	30 Ari	30 Tau	28 Gem	28 Can	29 Vir	28 Lib	30 Sag	28 Cap	29 Pis
30 Sag		31 Pis				31 Leo		30 Sco		30 Aqu	

1925

JAN.	FEB.	MAR.	APR.	MAY	JUN.	JUL.	AUG.	SEP.	OCT.	NOV.	DEC.
1 Ari	2 Gem	1 Gem	2 Leo	2 Vir	1 Lib	1 Sco	1 Cap	2 Pis	1 Ari	2 Gem	2 Can
3 Tau	4 Can	4 Can	5 Vir	5 Lib	3 Sco	3 Sag	3 Aqu	4 Ari	3 Tau	4 Can	4 Leo
5 Gem	7 Leo	6 Leo	7 Lib	7 Sco	5 Sag	5 Cap	5 Pis	6 Tau	6 Gem	7 Leo	7 Vir
8 Can	9 Vir	9 Vir	9 Sco	9 Sag	7 Cap	7 Aqu	7 Ari	8 Gem	8 Can	9 Vir	9 Lib
11 Leo	12 Lib	11 Lib	12 Sag	11 Cap	9 Aqu	9 Pis	9 Tau	11 Can	10 Leo	12 Lib	12 Sco
13 Vir	14 Sco	13 Sco	14 Cap	13 Aqu	11 Pis	11 Ari	12 Gem	13 Leo	13 Vir	14 Sco	14 Sag
15 Lib	16 Sag	15 Sag	16 Aqu	15 Pis	14 Ari	13 Tau	14 Can	16 Vir	15 Lib	16 Sag	16 Cap
18 Sco	18 Cap	17 Cap	18 Pis	17 Ari	16 Tau	16 Gem	17 Leo	18 Lib	18 Sco	18 Cap	18 Aqu
20 Sag	20 Aqu	20 Aqu	20 Ari	20 Tau	18 Gem	18 Can	19 Vir	20 Sco	20 Sag	20 Aqu	20 Pis
22 Cap	22 Pis	22 Pis	22 Tau	22 Gem	21 Can	21 Leo	22 Lib	23 Sag	22 Cap	23 Pis	22 Ari
24 Aqu	24 Ari	24 Ari	25 Gem	25 Can	23 Leo	23 Vir	24 Sco	25 Cap	24 Aqu	25 Ari	24 Tau
26 Pis	27 Tau	26 Tau	27 Can	27 Leo	26 Vir	26 Lib	26 Sag	27 Aqu	26 Pis	27 Tau	27 Gem
28 Ari		28 Gem	30 Leo	30 Vir	28 Lib	28 Sco	29 Cap	29 Pis	28 Ari	29 Gem	29 Can
30 Tau		31 Can				30 Sag	31 Aqu		31 Tau		31 Leo

1926

JAN.	FEB.	MAR.	APR.	MAY	JUN.	JUL.	AUG.	SEP.	OCT.	NOV.	DEC.
3 Vir	2 Lib	1 Lib	2 Sag	1 Cap	2 Pis	1 Ari	2 Gem	1 Can	3 Vir	2 Lib	1 Sco
5 Lib	4 Sco	3 Sco	4 Cap	4 Aqu	4 Ari	3 Tau	4 Can	3 Leo	5 Lib	4 Sco	4 Sag
8 Sco	7 Sag	6 Sag	6 Aqu	6 Pis	6 Tau	6 Gem	7 Leo	6 Vir	8 Sco	6 Sag	6 Cap
10 Sag	9 Cap	8 Cap	9 Pis	8 Ari	8 Gem	8 Can	9 Vir	8 Lib	10 Sag	9 Cap	8 Aqu
12 Cap	11 Aqu	10 Aqu	11 Ari	10 Tau	11 Can	11 Leo	12 Lib	11 Sco	13 Cap	11 Aqu	10 Pis
14 Aqu	13 Pis	12 Pis	13 Tau	12 Gem	13 Leo	13 Vir	14 Sco	13 Sag	15 Aqu	13 Pis	13 Ari
16 Pis	15 Ari	14 Ari	15 Gem	14 Can	16 Vir	16 Lib	17 Sag	15 Cap	17 Pis	15 Ari	15 Tau
18 Ari	17 Tau	16 Tau	17 Can	17 Leo	18 Lib	18 Sco	19 Cap	17 Aqu	19 Ari	17 Tau	17 Gem
20 Tau	19 Gem	18 Gem	20 Leo	19 Vir	21 Sco	20 Sag	21 Aqu	20 Pis	21 Tau	19 Gem	19 Can
23 Gem	21 Can	21 Can	22 Vir	22 Lib	23 Sag	23 Cap	23 Pis	21 Ari	23 Gem	22 Can	21 Leo
25 Can	24 Leo	23 Leo	25 Lib	24 Sco	25 Cap	25 Aqu	25 Ari	23 Tau	25 Can	24 Leo	24 Vir
28 Leo	26 Vir	26 Vir	27 Sco	27 Sag	27 Aqu	27 Pis	27 Tau	26 Gem	28 Leo	26 Vir	26 Lib
30 Vir		28 Lib	29 Sag	29 Cap	29 Pis	29 Ari	29 Gem	28 Can	30 Vir	29 Lib	29 Sco
		31 Sco		31 Aqu		31 Tau		30 Leo			31 Sag

1927

JAN.	FEB.	MAR.	APR.	MAY	JUN.	JUL.	AUG.	SEP.	OCT.	NOV.	DEC.
2 Cap	1 Aqu	3 Pis	1 Ari	2 Gem	1 Can	1 Leo	2 Lib	1 Sco	3 Cap	1 Aqu	1 Pis
5 Aqu	3 Pis	4 Ari	3 Tau	4 Can	3 Leo	3 Vir	4 Sco	3 Sag	5 Aqu	4 Pis	3 Ari
7 Pis	5 Ari	6 Tau	5 Gem	7 Leo	6 Vir	5 Lib	7 Sag	5 Cap	7 Pis	6 Ari	5 Tau
9 Ari	7 Tau	9 Gem	7 Can	9 Vir	8 Lib	8 Sco	9 Cap	8 Aqu	9 Ari	8 Tau	7 Gem
11 Tau	9 Gem	11 Can	9 Leo	12 Lib	11 Sco	10 Sag	11 Aqu	10 Pis	11 Tau	10 Gem	9 Can
13 Gem	12 Can	13 Leo	12 Vir	14 Sco	13 Sag	13 Cap	13 Pis	12 Ari	13 Gem	12 Can	11 Leo
15 Can	14 Leo	16 Vir	14 Lib	17 Sag	15 Cap	15 Aqu	15 Ari	14 Tau	15 Can	14 Leo	14 Vir
18 Leo	16 Vir	18 Lib	17 Sco	19 Cap	18 Aqu	17 Pis	18 Tau	16 Gem	18 Leo	16 Vir	16 Lib
20 Vir	19 Lib	21 Sco	19 Sag	21 Aqu	20 Pis	19 Ari	20 Gem	18 Can	20 Vir	19 Lib	19 Sco
23 Lib	21 Sco	23 Sag	22 Cap	24 Pis	22 Ari	21 Tau	22 Can	20 Leo	23 Lib	21 Sco	21 Sag
25 Sco	24 Sag	26 Cap	24 Aqu	26 Ari	24 Tau	23 Gem	24 Leo	23 Vir	25 Sco	24 Sag	24 Cap
28 Sag	26 Cap	28 Aqu	26 Pis	28 Tau	26 Gem	26 Can	27 Vir	25 Lib	28 Sag	26 Cap	26 Aqu
30 Cap	28 Aqu	30 Pis	28 Ari	30 Gem	28 Can	28 Leo	29 Lib	28 Sco	30 Cap	29 Aqu	28 Pis
			30 Tau			30 Vir		30 Sag			30 Ari

1928

JAN.	FEB.	MAR.	APR.	MAY	JUN.	JUL.	AUG.	SEP.	OCT.	NOV.	DEC.
1 Tau	2 Can	2 Leo	1 Vir	1 Lib	2 Sag	2 Cap	3 Pis	1 Ari	1 Tau	1 Can	1 Leo
4 Gem	4 Leo	5 Vir	3 Lib	3 Sco	4 Cap	4 Aqu	5 Ari	3 Tau	3 Gem	2 Leo	3 Vir
6 Can	6 Vir	7 Lib	6 Sco	6 Sag	7 Aqu	6 Pis	7 Tau	5 Gem	5 Can	5 Vir	5 Lib
8 Leo	9 Lib	10 Sco	8 Sag	8 Cap	9 Pis	9 Ari	9 Gem	8 Can	7 Leo	8 Lib	7 Sco
10 Vir	11 Sco	12 Sag	11 Cap	11 Aqu	11 Ari	11 Tau	11 Can	10 Leo	9 Vir	10 Sco	10 Sag
12 Lib	14 Sag	15 Cap	13 Aqu	13 Pis	14 Tau	13 Gem	13 Leo	12 Vir	12 Lib	13 Sag	13 Cap
15 Sco	16 Cap	17 Aqu	16 Pis	15 Ari	16 Gem	15 Can	16 Vir	14 Lib	14 Sco	15 Cap	15 Aqu
17 Sag	19 Aqu	19 Pis	18 Ari	17 Tau	18 Can	17 Leo	18 Lib	17 Sco	16 Sag	18 Aqu	17 Pis
20 Cap	21 Pis	21 Ari	20 Tau	19 Gem	20 Leo	19 Vir	20 Sco	19 Sag	19 Cap	20 Pis	20 Ari
22 Aqu	23 Ari	23 Tau	22 Gem	21 Can	22 Vir	22 Lib	23 Sag	22 Cap	22 Aqu	22 Ari	22 Tau
24 Pis	25 Tau	25 Gem	24 Can	23 Leo	24 Lib	24 Sco	25 Cap	24 Aqu	24 Pis	25 Tau	24 Gem
27 Ari	27 Gem	27 Can	26 Leo	26 Vir	27 Sco	27 Sag	28 Aqu	26 Pis	26 Ari	27 Gem	26 Can
29 Tau	29 Can	30 Leo	28 Vir	28 Lib	29 Sag	29 Cap	30 Pis	29 Ari	28 Tau	29 Can	28 Leo
31 Gem				30 Sco		31 Aqu			30 Gem		30 Vir

1929

JAN.	FEB.	MAR.	APR.	MAY	JUN.	JUL.	AUG.	SEP.	OCT.	NOV.	DEC.
1 Lib	3 Sag	2 Sag	1 Cap	1 Aqu	2 Ari	1 Tau	2 Can	2 Vir	2 Lib	3 Sag	2 Cap
4 Sco	5 Cap	4 Cap	3 Aqu	3 Pis	4 Tau	3 Gem	4 Leo	4 Lib	4 Sco	5 Cap	5 Aqu
6 Sag	8 Aqu	7 Aqu	6 Pis	5 Ari	6 Gem	5 Can	6 Vir	7 Sco	6 Sag	8 Aqu	8 Pis
9 Cap	10 Pis	9 Pis	8 Ari	8 Tau	8 Can	7 Leo	8 Lib	9 Sag	9 Cap	10 Pis	10 Ari
11 Aqu	12 Ari	12 Ari	10 Tau	10 Gem	10 Leo	9 Vir	10 Sco	11 Cap	11 Aqu	13 Ari	12 Tau
14 Pis	15 Tau	14 Tau	12 Gem	12 Can	12 Vir	12 Lib	13 Sag	14 Aqu	14 Pis	15 Tau	14 Gem
16 Ari	17 Gem	16 Gem	14 Can	14 Leo	14 Lib	14 Sco	15 Cap	16 Pis	16 Ari	17 Gem	16 Can
18 Tau	19 Can	18 Can	16 Leo	16 Vir	17 Sco	16 Sag	18 Aqu	19 Ari	18 Tau	19 Can	18 Leo
20 Gem	21 Leo	20 Leo	19 Vir	18 Lib	19 Sag	19 Cap	20 Pis	21 Tau	21 Gem	21 Leo	20 Vir
22 Can	23 Vir	22 Vir	21 Lib	20 Sco	22 Cap	21 Aqu	23 Ari	23 Gem	23 Can	23 Vir	23 Lib
24 Leo	25 Lib	25 Lib	23 Sco	23 Sag	24 Aqu	24 Pis	25 Tau	25 Can	25 Leo	25 Lib	25 Sco
27 Vir	27 Sco	27 Sco	26 Sag	25 Cap	27 Pis	26 Ari	27 Gem	28 Leo	27 Vir	28 Sco	27 Sag
29 Lib		29 Sag	28 Cap	28 Aqu	29 Ari	29 Tau	29 Can	30 Vir	29 Lib	30 Sag	30 Cap
31 Sco				30 Pis		31 Gem	31 Leo		31 Sco		

52

1930

JAN.	FEB.	MAR.	APR.	MAY	JUN.	JUL.	AUG.	SEP.	OCT.	NOV.	DEC.
1 Aqu	3 Ari	2 Ari	3 Gem	2 Can	3 Vir	2 Lib	3 Sag	1 Cap	1 Aqu	2 Ari	2 Tau
4 Pis	5 Tau	4 Tau	5 Can	4 Leo	5 Lib	4 Sco	5 Cap	4 Aqu	4 Pis	5 Tau	5 Gem
6 Ari	7 Gem	6 Gem	7 Leo	6 Vir	7 Sco	6 Sag	8 Aqu	6 Pis	6 Ari	7 Gem	7 Can
9 Tau	9 Can	9 Can	9 Vir	8 Lib	9 Sag	9 Cap	10 Pis	9 Ari	9 Tau	9 Can	9 Leo
11 Gem	11 Leo	11 Leo	11 Lib	11 Sco	12 Cap	11 Aqu	13 Ari	11 Tau	11 Gem	12 Leo	11 Vir
13 Can	13 Vir	13 Vir	13 Sco	13 Sag	14 Aqu	14 Pis	15 Tau	14 Gem	13 Can	14 Vir	13 Lib
15 Leo	15 Lib	15 Lib	16 Sag	15 Cap	17 Pis	16 Ari	17 Gem	16 Can	15 Leo	16 Lib	15 Sco
17 Vir	17 Sco	17 Sco	18 Cap	18 Aqu	19 Ari	19 Tau	20 Can	18 Leo	17 Vir	18 Sco	17 Sag
19 Lib	20 Sag	19 Sag	20 Aqu	20 Pis	21 Tau	21 Gem	22 Leo	20 Lib	19 Lib	20 Sag	20 Cap
21 Sco	22 Cap	22 Cap	23 Pis	23 Ari	24 Gem	23 Can	24 Vir	22 Lib	22 Sco	22 Cap	22 Aqu
23 Sag	25 Aqu	24 Aqu	25 Ari	25 Tau	26 Can	25 Leo	26 Lib	24 Sco	24 Sag	25 Aqu	25 Pis
26 Cap	27 Pis	27 Pis	28 Tau	27 Gem	28 Leo	27 Vir	28 Sco	26 Sag	26 Cap	27 Pis	27 Ari
29 Aqu		29 Ari	30 Gem	29 Can	30 Vir	29 Lib	30 Sag	29 Cap	28 Aqu	30 Ari	30 Tau
31 Pis		31 Tau		31 Leo		31 Sco			31 Pis		

1931

JAN.	FEB.	MAR.	APR.	MAY	JUN.	JUL.	AUG.	SEP.	OCT.	NOV.	DEC.
1 Gem	2 Leo	1 Leo	2 Lib	1 Sco	2 Cap	1 Aqu	3 Ari	1 Tau	1 Gem	2 Leo	2 Vir
3 Can	4 Vir	3 Vir	4 Sco	3 Sag	4 Aqu	4 Pis	5 Tau	4 Gem	4 Can	4 Vir	4 Lib
5 Leo	6 Lib	5 Lib	6 Sag	5 Cap	6 Pis	6 Ari	8 Gem	6 Can	6 Leo	6 Lib	6 Sco
7 Vir	8 Sco	7 Sco	8 Cap	8 Aqu	9 Ari	9 Tau	10 Can	8 Leo	8 Vir	8 Sco	8 Sag
9 Lib	10 Sag	9 Sag	10 Aqu	10 Pis	11 Tau	11 Gem	12 Leo	10 Vir	10 Lib	10 Sag	10 Cap
11 Sco	12 Cap	12 Cap	13 Pis	13 Ari	14 Gem	13 Can	14 Vir	12 Lib	12 Sco	12 Cap	12 Aqu
14 Sag	15 Aqu	14 Aqu	15 Ari	15 Tau	16 Can	16 Leo	16 Lib	14 Sco	14 Sag	15 Aqu	14 Pis
16 Cap	17 Pis	16 Pis	18 Tau	17 Gem	18 Leo	18 Lib	18 Sco	17 Sag	16 Cap	17 Pis	17 Ari
18 Aqu	20 Ari	19 Ari	20 Gem	20 Can	20 Vir	20 Lib	20 Sag	19 Cap	18 Aqu	20 Ari	19 Tau
21 Pis	22 Tau	22 Tau	23 Can	22 Leo	22 Lib	22 Sco	22 Cap	21 Aqu	21 Pis	22 Tau	22 Gem
23 Ari	25 Gem	24 Gem	25 Leo	24 Vir	25 Sco	24 Sag	25 Aqu	24 Pis	23 Ari	25 Gem	24 Can
26 Tau	27 Can	26 Can	27 Vir	26 Lib	27 Sag	26 Cap	27 Pis	26 Ari	26 Tau	27 Can	27 Leo
28 Gem		28 Leo	29 Lib	28 Sco	29 Cap	29 Aqu	30 Ari	29 Tau	28 Gem	29 Leo	29 Vir
31 Can		31 Vir		30 Sag		31 Pis			31 Can		31 Lib

53

1932

JAN.	FEB.	MAR.	APR.	MAY	JUN.	JUL.	AUG.	SEP.	OCT.	NOV.	DEC.
2 Sco	3 Cap	1 Cap	2 Pis	1 Ari	3 Gem	3 Can	1 Leo	2 Lib	1 Sco	2 Cap	1 Aqu
4 Sag	5 Aqu	3 Aqu	4 Ari	4 Tau	5 Can	5 Leo	3 Vir	4 Sco	3 Sag	4 Aqu	3 Pis
6 Cap	7 Pis	5 Pis	7 Tau	7 Gem	8 Leo	7 Vir	6 Lib	6 Sag	5 Cap	6 Pis	6 Ari
8 Aqu	10 Ari	8 Ari	9 Gem	9 Can	10 Vir	9 Lib	8 Sco	8 Cap	8 Aqu	9 Ari	8 Tau
11 Pis	12 Tau	10 Tau	12 Can	11 Leo	12 Lib	11 Sco	10 Sag	10 Aqu	10 Pis	11 Tau	11 Gem
13 Ari	15 Gem	13 Gem	14 Leo	14 Vir	14 Sco	14 Sag	12 Cap	13 Pis	12 Ari	14 Gem	13 Can
16 Tau	17 Can	15 Can	16 Vir	16 Lib	16 Sag	16 Cap	14 Aqu	15 Ari	15 Tau	16 Can	16 Leo
18 Gem	19 Leo	18 Leo	18 Lib	18 Sco	18 Cap	18 Aqu	16 Pis	18 Tau	17 Gem	19 Leo	18 Vir
21 Can	21 Vir	20 Vir	20 Sco	20 Sag	20 Aqu	20 Pis	19 Ari	20 Gem	20 Can	21 Vir	20 Lib
23 Leo	23 Lib	22 Lib	22 Sag	22 Cap	23 Pis	22 Ari	21 Tau	23 Can	22 Leo	23 Lib	23 Sco
25 Vir	26 Sco	24 Sco	24 Cap	24 Aqu	25 Ari	25 Tau	24 Gem	25 Leo	25 Vir	25 Sco	25 Sag
27 Lib	28 Sag	26 Sag	27 Aqu	26 Pis	28 Tau	27 Gem	26 Can	27 Vir	27 Lib	27 Sag	27 Cap
29 Sco		28 Cap	29 Pis	29 Ari	30 Gem	30 Can	29 Leo	29 Lib	29 Sco	29 Cap	29 Aqu
31 Sag		30 Aqu		31 Tau			31 Vir		31 Sag		31 Pis

1933

JAN.	FEB.	MAR.	APR.	MAY	JUN.	JUL.	AUG.	SEP.	OCT.	NOV.	DEC.
2 Ari	1 Tau	3 Gem	2 Can	1 Leo	2 Lib	2 Sco	2 Cap	1 Aqu	2 Ari	1 Tau	1 Gem
5 Tau	3 Gem	5 Can	4 Leo	4 Vir	5 Sco	4 Sag	4 Aqu	3 Pis	5 Tau	4 Gem	3 Can
7 Gem	6 Can	8 Leo	6 Vir	6 Lib	7 Sag	6 Cap	7 Pis	5 Ari	7 Gem	6 Can	6 Leo
10 Can	8 Leo	10 Vir	9 Lib	8 Sco	9 Cap	8 Aqu	9 Ari	7 Tau	10 Can	9 Leo	8 Vir
12 Leo	11 Vir	12 Lib	11 Sco	10 Sag	11 Aqu	10 Pis	11 Tau	10 Gem	12 Leo	11 Vir	11 Lib
14 Vir	13 Lib	14 Sco	13 Sag	12 Cap	13 Pis	12 Ari	13 Gem	12 Can	15 Vir	13 Lib	13 Sco
17 Lib	15 Sco	16 Sag	15 Cap	14 Aqu	15 Ari	15 Tau	16 Can	15 Leo	17 Lib	15 Sco	15 Sag
19 Sco	17 Sag	19 Cap	17 Aqu	16 Pis	17 Tau	17 Gem	19 Leo	17 Vir	19 Sco	18 Sag	17 Cap
21 Sag	19 Cap	21 Aqu	19 Pis	19 Ari	20 Gem	20 Can	21 Vir	20 Lib	21 Sag	20 Cap	19 Aqu
23 Cap	21 Aqu	23 Pis	22 Ari	21 Tau	22 Can	22 Leo	23 Lib	22 Sco	23 Cap	22 Aqu	21 Pis
25 Aqu	24 Pis	25 Ari	24 Tau	24 Gem	25 Leo	25 Vir	25 Sco	24 Sag	25 Aqu	24 Pis	23 Ari
27 Pis	26 Ari	28 Tau	26 Gem	26 Can	27 Vir	27 Lib	28 Sag	26 Cap	27 Pis	26 Ari	26 Tau
30 Ari	28 Tau	30 Gem	29 Can	29 Leo	30 Lib	29 Sco	30 Cap	28 Aqu	30 Ari	28 Tau	28 Gem
				31 Vir		31 Sag		30 Pis			31 Can

1934

JAN.	FEB.	MAR.	APR.	MAY	JUN.	JUL.	AUG.	SEP.	OCT.	NOV.	DEC.
2 Leo	1 Vir	3 Lib	1 Sco	1 Sag	1 Aqu	3 Ari	1 Tau	2 Can	2 Leo	1 Vir	1 Lib
5 Vir	3 Lib	5 Sco	3 Sag	3 Cap	3 Pis	5 Tau	3 Gem	5 Leo	5 Vir	3 Lib	3 Sco
7 Lib	6 Sco	7 Sag	5 Cap	5 Aqu	5 Ari	7 Gem	6 Can	7 Vir	7 Lib	6 Sco	5 Sag
9 Sco	8 Sag	9 Cap	7 Aqu	7 Pis	8 Tau	10 Can	8 Leo	10 Lib	9 Sco	8 Sag	7 Cap
11 Sag	10 Cap	11 Aqu	10 Pis	9 Ari	10 Gem	12 Leo	11 Vir	12 Sco	12 Sag	10 Cap	9 Aqu
13 Cap	12 Aqu	13 Pis	12 Ari	11 Tau	12 Can	15 Vir	13 Lib	14 Sag	14 Cap	12 Aqu	11 Pis
15 Aqu	14 Pis	15 Ari	14 Tau	14 Gem	15 Leo	17 Lib	16 Sco	17 Cap	16 Aqu	14 Pis	14 Ari
17 Pis	16 Ari	18 Tau	16 Gem	16 Can	17 Vir	20 Sco	18 Sag	19 Aqu	18 Pis	16 Ari	16 Tau
20 Ari	18 Tau	20 Gem	19 Can	19 Leo	20 Lib	22 Sag	20 Cap	21 Pis	20 Ari	19 Tau	18 Gem
22 Tau	21 Gem	22 Can	21 Vir	21 Vir	22 Sco	24 Cap	22 Aqu	23 Ari	22 Tau	21 Gem	21 Can
24 Gem	23 Can	25 Leo	24 Vir	24 Lib	24 Sag	26 Aqu	24 Pis	25 Tau	24 Gem	23 Can	23 Leo
27 Can	26 Leo	27 Vir	26 Lib	26 Sco	26 Cap	28 Pis	26 Ari	27 Gem	27 Can	26 Leo	26 Vir
29 Leo	28 Vir	30 Lib	28 Sco	28 Sag	28 Aqu	30 Ari	28 Tau	29 Can	29 Leo	28 Vir	28 Lib
				30 Cap	30 Pis		31 Gem				30 Sco

1935

JAN.	FEB.	MAR.	APR.	MAY	JUN.	JUL.	AUG.	SEP.	OCT.	NOV.	DEC.
2 Sag	2 Aqu	2 Aqu	2 Ari	2 Tau	2 Can	2 Leo	1 Vir	2 Sco	2 Sag	3 Aqu	2 Pis
4 Cap	4 Pis	4 Pis	4 Tau	4 Gem	5 Leo	5 Vir	3 Lib	5 Sag	4 Cap	5 Pis	4 Ari
6 Aqu	6 Ari	6 Ari	6 Gem	6 Can	7 Vir	7 Lib	6 Sco	7 Cap	6 Aqu	7 Ari	6 Tau
8 Pis	8 Tau	8 Tau	9 Can	8 Leo	10 Lib	10 Sco	8 Sag	9 Aqu	9 Pis	9 Tau	8 Gem
10 Ari	11 Gem	10 Gem	11 Leo	11 Vir	12 Sco	12 Sag	11 Cap	11 Pis	11 Ari	11 Gem	11 Can
12 Tau	13 Can	12 Can	14 Vir	13 Lib	15 Sag	14 Cap	13 Aqu	13 Ari	12 Tau	13 Can	13 Leo
14 Gem	16 Leo	15 Leo	16 Lib	16 Sco	17 Cap	16 Aqu	15 Pis	15 Tau	15 Gem	15 Leo	15 Vir
17 Can	18 Vir	17 Vir	19 Sco	18 Sag	19 Aqu	18 Pis	17 Ari	17 Gem	17 Can	18 Vir	18 Lib
19 Leo	21 Lib	20 Lib	21 Sag	20 Cap	21 Pis	20 Ari	19 Tau	19 Can	19 Leo	20 Lib	20 Sco
22 Vir	23 Sco	22 Sco	23 Cap	23 Aqu	23 Ari	22 Tau	21 Gem	22 Leo	22 Vir	23 Sco	23 Sag
24 Lib	25 Sag	25 Sag	25 Aqu	25 Pis	25 Tau	25 Gem	23 Can	24 Vir	24 Lib	25 Sag	25 Cap
27 Sco	28 Cap	27 Cap	27 Pis	27 Ari	27 Gem	27 Can	26 Leo	27 Lib	27 Sco	28 Cap	27 Aqu
29 Sag		29 Aqu	30 Ari	29 Tau	30 Can	29 Leo	28 Vir	29 Sco	29 Sag	30 Aqu	29 Pis
31 Cap		31 Pis		31 Gem			31 Lib		31 Cap		31 Ari

55

1936

JAN.	FEB.	MAR.	APR.	MAY	JUN.	JUL.	AUG.	SEP.	OCT.	NOV.	DEC.
3 Tau	1 Gem	1 Can	3 Vir	2 Lib	1 Sco	1 Sag	2 Aqu	2 Ari	2 Tau	2 Can	2 Leo
5 Gem	3 Can	4 Leo	5 Lib	5 Sco	4 Sag	3 Cap	4 Pis	4 Tau	4 Gem	5 Leo	4 Vir
7 Can	6 Leo	6 Vir	8 Sco	7 Sag	6 Cap	6 Aqu	6 Ari	7 Gem	6 Can	7 Vir	7 Lib
9 Leo	8 Vir	9 Lib	10 Sag	10 Cap	8 Aqu	8 Pis	8 Tau	9 Can	8 Leo	9 Lib	9 Sco
12 Vir	10 Lib	11 Sco	12 Cap	12 Aqu	10 Pis	10 Ari	10 Gem	11 Leo	11 Vir	12 Sco	12 Sag
14 Lib	13 Sco	14 Sag	15 Aqu	14 Pis	13 Ari	12 Tau	12 Can	13 Vir	13 Lib	14 Sag	14 Cap
17 Sco	15 Sag	16 Cap	17 Pis	16 Ari	15 Tau	14 Gem	15 Leo	16 Lib	16 Sco	17 Cap	17 Aqu
19 Sag	18 Cap	18 Aqu	19 Ari	18 Tau	17 Gem	16 Can	17 Vir	18 Sco	18 Sag	19 Aqu	19 Pis
21 Cap	20 Aqu	21 Pis	21 Tau	20 Gem	19 Can	18 Leo	20 Lib	21 Sag	21 Cap	22 Pis	21 Ari
24 Aqu	22 Pis	23 Ari	23 Gem	22 Can	21 Leo	21 Vir	22 Sco	23 Cap	23 Aqu	24 Ari	23 Tau
26 Pis	24 Ari	24 Tau	25 Can	25 Leo	23 Vir	23 Lib	25 Sag	26 Aqu	25 Pis	26 Tau	25 Gem
28 Ari	26 Tau	27 Gem	27 Leo	27 Vir	26 Lib	26 Sco	27 Cap	28 Pis	27 Ari	28 Gem	27 Can
30 Tau	28 Gem	29 Can	30 Vir	30 Lib	28 Sco	28 Sag	29 Aqu	30 Ari	29 Tau	30 Can	29 Leo
		31 Leo				31 Cap	31 Pis		31 Gem		31 Cap

1937

JAN.	FEB.	MAR.	APR.	MAY	JUN.	JUL.	AUG.	SEP.	OCT.	NOV.	DEC.
1 Vir	2 Sco	1 Sco	3 Cap	2 Aqu	1 Pis	3 Tau	1 Gem	1 Leo	1 Vir	2 Sco	2 Sag
3 Lib	4 Sag	4 Sag	5 Aqu	5 Pis	3 Ari	5 Gem	3 Can	4 Vir	3 Lib	4 Sag	4 Cap
5 Sco	7 Cap	6 Cap	7 Pis	7 Ari	5 Tau	7 Can	5 Leo	6 Lib	6 Sco	7 Cap	7 Aqu
8 Sag	9 Aqu	9 Aqu	9 Ari	9 Tau	7 Gem	9 Leo	7 Vir	8 Sco	8 Sag	9 Aqu	9 Pis
10 Cap	11 Pis	11 Pis	11 Tau	11 Gem	9 Can	11 Vir	9 Lib	11 Sag	11 Cap	12 Pis	11 Ari
13 Aqu	14 Ari	13 Ari	13 Gem	13 Can	11 Leo	13 Lib	12 Sco	13 Cap	13 Aqu	14 Ari	14 Tau
15 Pis	16 Tau	15 Tau	15 Can	15 Leo	13 Vir	16 Sco	14 Sag	16 Aqu	15 Pis	16 Tau	16 Gem
17 Ari	18 Gem	17 Gem	18 Leo	17 Vir	16 Lib	18 Sag	17 Cap	18 Pis	18 Ari	18 Gem	18 Can
19 Tau	20 Can	19 Can	20 Vir	19 Lib	18 Sco	21 Cap	19 Aqu	20 Ari	20 Tau	20 Can	20 Leo
21 Gem	22 Leo	21 Leo	22 Lib	22 Sco	21 Sag	23 Aqu	22 Pis	22 Tau	22 Gem	22 Leo	22 Vir
24 Can	24 Vir	24 Vir	25 Sco	25 Sag	23 Cap	25 Pis	24 Ari	24 Gem	24 Can	24 Vir	24 Lib
26 Leo	27 Lib	26 Lib	27 Sag	27 Cap	26 Aqu	28 Ari	26 Tau	26 Can	26 Leo	27 Lib	26 Sco
28 Vir		28 Sco	30 Cap	30 Aqu	28 Pis	30 Tau	28 Gem	29 Leo	28 Vir	29 Sco	29 Sag
30 Lib		31 Sag			30 Ari		30 Can		30 Lib		31 Cap

1938

JAN.	FEB.	MAR.	APR.	MAY	JUN.	JUL.	AUG.	SEP.	OCT.	NOV.	DEC.
3 Aqu	2 Pis	1 Pis	2 Tau	1 Gem	2 Leo	1 Vir	2 Sco	1 Sag	3 Aqu	2 Pis	1 Ari
5 Pis	4 Ari	3 Ari	4 Gem	3 Can	4 Vir	3 Lib	4 Sag	3 Cap	5 Pis	4 Ari	4 Tau
8 Ari	6 Tau	5 Tau	6 Can	5 Leo	6 Lib	5 Sco	7 Cap	6 Aqu	8 Ari	6 Tau	6 Gem
10 Tau	8 Gem	8 Gem	8 Leo	7 Vir	8 Sco	8 Sag	9 Aqu	8 Pis	10 Tau	9 Gem	8 Can
12 Gem	10 Can	10 Can	10 Vir	10 Lib	11 Sag	10 Cap	12 Pis	10 Ari	12 Gem	11 Can	10 Leo
14 Can	12 Leo	12 Leo	12 Lib	12 Sco	13 Cap	13 Aqu	14 Ari	13 Tau	14 Can	13 Leo	12 Vir
16 Leo	15 Vir	14 Vir	15 Sco	14 Sag	16 Aqu	15 Pis	16 Tau	15 Gem	16 Leo	15 Vir	14 Lib
18 Vir	17 Lib	16 Lib	17 Sag	17 Cap	18 Pis	18 Ari	19 Gem	17 Can	19 Lib	17 Lib	16 Sco
20 Lib	19 Sco	18 Sco	20 Cap	19 Aqu	21 Ari	20 Tau	21 Can	19 Leo	21 Lib	19 Sco	19 Sag
23 Sco	21 Sag	21 Sag	22 Aqu	22 Pis	23 Tau	22 Gem	23 Leo	21 Vir	23 Sco	22 Sag	21 Cap
25 Sag	24 Cap	23 Cap	25 Pis	24 Ari	25 Gem	24 Can	25 Vir	23 Lib	25 Sag	24 Cap	24 Aqu
28 Cap	26 Aqu	26 Aqu	27 Ari	27 Tau	27 Can	26 Leo	27 Lib	26 Sco	28 Cap	27 Aqu	26 Pis
30 Aqu		28 Pis	29 Tau	29 Gem	29 Leo	28 Vir	29 Sco	28 Sag	30 Aqu	29 Pis	29 Ari
		31 Ari		31 Can		31 Lib		30 Cap			31 Tau

1939

JAN.	FEB.	MAR.	APR.	MAY	JUN.	JUL.	AUG.	SEP.	OCT.	NOV.	DEC.
2 Gem	1 Can	2 Leo	1 Vir	2 Sco	1 Sag	3 Aqu	2 Pis	3 Tau	3 Gem	1 Can	3 Vir
4 Can	3 Leo	4 Vir	3 Lib	4 Sag	3 Cap	5 Pis	4 Ari	5 Gem	5 Can	3 Leo	5 Lib
6 Leo	5 Sco	6 Lib	5 Sco	7 Cap	6 Aqu	8 Ari	7 Tau	8 Can	7 Leo	5 Vir	7 Sco
8 Vir	7 Lib	8 Sco	7 Sag	9 Aqu	8 Pis	10 Tau	9 Gem	10 Leo	9 Vir	7 Lib	9 Sag
10 Lib	9 Sco	11 Sag	9 Cap	12 Pis	11 Ari	13 Gem	11 Can	12 Vir	11 Lib	10 Sco	11 Cap
13 Sco	11 Sag	13 Cap	12 Aqu	14 Ari	13 Tau	15 Can	13 Leo	14 Lib	13 Sco	12 Sag	14 Aqu
15 Sag	14 Cap	16 Aqu	14 Pis	17 Tau	15 Gem	17 Leo	15 Vir	16 Sco	15 Sag	14 Cap	16 Pis
18 Cap	16 Aqu	18 Pis	17 Ari	19 Gem	17 Can	19 Vir	17 Lib	18 Sag	18 Cap	16 Aqu	19 Ari
20 Aqu	19 Pis	21 Ari	19 Tau	21 Leo	19 Leo	21 Lib	19 Sco	20 Cap	20 Aqu	19 Pis	21 Tau
23 Pis	21 Ari	23 Tau	22 Gem	23 Leo	21 Vir	23 Sco	22 Sag	23 Aqu	23 Pis	21 Ari	24 Gem
25 Ari	24 Tau	25 Gem	24 Can	25 Vir	24 Lib	25 Sag	24 Cap	25 Pis	25 Ari	24 Tau	26 Can
28 Tau	26 Gem	28 Can	26 Leo	27 Lib	26 Sco	28 Cap	26 Aqu	28 Ari	27 Tau	26 Gem	28 Leo
30 Gem	28 Can	30 Leo	28 Vir	30 Sco	28 Sag	30 Aqu	29 Pis	30 Tau	30 Gem	28 Can	30 Vir
			30 Lib		30 Cap		31 Ari			30 Leo	

1940

JAN.	FEB.	MAR.	APR.	MAY	JUN.	JUL.	AUG.	SEP.	OCT.	NOV.	DEC.
1 Lib	2 Sag	2 Cap	1 Aqu	1 Pis	2 Tau	2 Gem	3 Leo	1 Vir	2 Sco	1 Sag	3 Aqu
3 Sco	4 Cap	5 Aqu	3 Pis	3 Ari	4 Gem	4 Can	5 Vir	3 Lib	4 Sag	3 Cap	5 Pis
5 Sag	6 Aqu	7 Pis	6 Ari	6 Tau	7 Can	6 Leo	7 Lib	5 Sco	7 Cap	5 Aqu	7 Ari
8 Cap	9 Pis	10 Ari	8 Tau	8 Gem	9 Leo	8 Vir	9 Sco	7 Sag	9 Aqu	8 Pis	10 Tau
10 Aqu	11 Ari	12 Tau	11 Gem	10 Can	11 Vir	10 Lib	11 Sag	9 Cap	11 Pis	10 Ari	13 Gem
13 Pis	14 Tau	15 Gem	13 Can	13 Leo	13 Lib	13 Sco	13 Cap	12 Aqu	14 Ari	13 Tau	15 Can
15 Ari	16 Gem	17 Can	15 Leo	15 Vir	15 Sco	15 Sag	15 Aqu	14 Pis	16 Tau	15 Gem	17 Leo
18 Tau	19 Can	19 Leo	18 Vir	17 Lib	17 Sag	17 Cap	18 Pis	17 Ari	19 Gem	18 Can	19 Vir
20 Gem	21 Leo	21 Vir	20 Lib	19 Sco	20 Cap	19 Aqu	20 Ari	19 Tau	21 Can	20 Leo	22 Lib
22 Can	23 Vir	23 Lib	22 Sco	21 Sag	22 Aqu	22 Pis	23 Tau	22 Gem	24 Leo	22 Vir	24 Sco
24 Leo	25 Lib	25 Sco	24 Sag	23 Cap	24 Pis	24 Ari	25 Gem	24 Can	26 Vir	24 Lib	26 Sag
26 Vir	27 Sco	27 Sag	26 Cap	25 Aqu	27 Ari	27 Tau	28 Can	26 Leo	28 Lib	26 Sco	28 Cap
28 Lib	29 Sag	29 Cap	28 Aqu	28 Pis	29 Tau	29 Gem	30 Leo	28 Vir	30 Sco	28 Sag	30 Aqu
30 Sco				30 Ari		31 Can		30 Lib		30 Cap	

1941

JAN.	FEB.	MAR.	APR.	MAY	JUN.	JUL.	AUG.	SEP.	OCT.	NOV.	DEC.
1 Pis	3 Tau	2 Tau	1 Gem	1 Can	2 Vir	1 Lib	1 Sag	2 Aqu	2 Pis	3 Tau	2 Gem
4 Ari	5 Gem	5 Gem	3 Can	3 Leo	4 Lib	3 Sco	4 Cap	4 Pis	4 Ari	5 Gem	5 Can
6 Tau	8 Can	7 Can	6 Leo	5 Vir	6 Sco	5 Sag	6 Aqu	7 Ari	6 Tau	8 Can	7 Leo
9 Gem	10 Leo	9 Leo	8 Vir	7 Lib	8 Sag	7 Cap	8 Pis	9 Tau	9 Gem	10 Leo	10 Vir
11 Can	12 Vir	11 Vir	10 Lib	9 Sco	10 Cap	9 Aqu	10 Ari	12 Gem	11 Can	13 Vir	12 Lib
13 Leo	14 Lib	13 Lib	12 Sco	11 Sag	12 Aqu	12 Pis	13 Tau	14 Can	14 Leo	15 Lib	14 Sco
16 Vir	16 Sco	16 Sco	14 Sag	13 Cap	14 Pis	14 Ari	15 Gem	16 Leo	16 Vir	17 Sco	16 Sag
18 Lib	18 Sag	18 Sag	16 Cap	16 Aqu	17 Ari	16 Tau	18 Can	19 Vir	18 Lib	19 Sag	18 Cap
20 Sco	20 Cap	20 Cap	18 Aqu	18 Pis	19 Tau	19 Gem	20 Leo	21 Lib	20 Sco	21 Cap	20 Aqu
22 Sag	23 Aqu	22 Aqu	21 Pis	20 Ari	22 Gem	21 Can	22 Vir	23 Vir	22 Sag	23 Aqu	22 Pis
24 Cap	25 Pis	24 Pis	23 Ari	23 Tau	24 Can	24 Leo	24 Lib	25 Sag	24 Cap	25 Pis	25 Ari
26 Aqu	27 Ari	27 Ari	26 Tau	25 Gem	26 Leo	26 Vir	27 Sco	27 Cap	26 Aqu	27 Ari	27 Tau
29 Pis		29 Tau	28 Gem	28 Can	29 Vir	28 Lib	29 Sag	29 Aqu	29 Pis	30 Tau	30 Gem
31 Ari				30 Leo		30 Sco	31 Cap		31 Ari		

1941

JAN.	FEB.	MAR.	APR.	MAY	JUN.	JUL.	AUG.	SEP.	OCT.	NOV.	DEC.
1 Can	2 Vir	2 Vir	2 Sco	2 Sag	2 Aqu	2 Pis	3 Tau	1 Gem	1 Can	3 Vir	2 Lib
4 Leo	5 Lib	4 Lib	4 Sag	4 Cap	4 Pis	4 Ari	5 Gem	4 Can	4 Leo	5 Lib	4 Sco
6 Vir	7 Sco	6 Sco	6 Cap	6 Aqu	7 Ari	6 Tau	8 Can	6 Leo	6 Vir	7 Sco	7 Sag
8 Lib	9 Sag	8 Sag	9 Aqu	8 Pis	9 Tau	9 Gem	10 Leo	9 Vir	8 Lib	9 Sag	9 Cap
11 Sco	11 Cap	10 Cap	11 Pis	10 Ari	12 Gem	11 Can	13 Vir	11 Lib	11 Sco	11 Cap	11 Aqu
13 Sag	13 Aqu	12 Aqu	13 Ari	13 Tau	14 Can	14 Leo	15 Lib	13 Sco	13 Sag	13 Aqu	13 Pis
15 Cap	15 Pis	15 Pis	16 Tau	15 Gem	17 Leo	16 Vir	17 Sco	15 Sag	15 Cap	15 Pis	15 Ari
17 Aqu	17 Ari	17 Ari	18 Gem	16 Can	19 Vir	19 Lib	19 Sag	18 Cap	17 Aqu	18 Ari	17 Tau
19 Pis	20 Tau	19 Tau	21 Can	20 Leo	21 Lib	21 Sco	21 Cap	20 Aqu	19 Pis	20 Tau	20 Gem
21 Ari	22 Gem	22 Gem	23 Leo	23 Vir	24 Sco	23 Sag	23 Aqu	22 Pis	21 Ari	22 Gem	22 Can
23 Tau	25 Can	24 Can	25 Vir	25 Lib	26 Sag	25 Cap	25 Pis	24 Ari	24 Tau	25 Can	25 Leo
26 Gem	26 Leo	27 Leo	28 Lib	27 Sco	28 Cap	27 Aqu	28 Ari	26 Tau	26 Gem	27 Leo	27 Vir
29 Can		29 Vir	30 Sco	29 Sag	30 Aqu	29 Pis	30 Tau	29 Gem	29 Can	30 Vir	30 Lib
31 Leo		31 Lib		31 Cap		31 Ari			31 Leo		

1943

JAN.	FEB.	MAR.	APR.	MAY	JUN.	JUL.	AUG.	SEP.	OCT.	NOV.	DEC.
1 Sco	1 Cap	1 Cap	1 Pis	1 Ari	2 Gem	1 Can	3 Vir	1 Lib	1 Sco	2 Cap	1 Aqu
3 Sag	3 Aqu	3 Aqu	3 Ari	3 Tau	4 Can	4 Leo	5 Lib	4 Sco	3 Sag	4 Aqu	3 Pis
5 Cap	5 Pis	5 Pis	6 Tau	5 Gem	6 Leo	6 Vir	7 Sco	6 Sag	5 Cap	6 Pis	5 Ari
7 Aqu	8 Ari	7 Ari	8 Gem	8 Can	9 Vir	9 Lib	10 Sag	8 Cap	8 Aqu	8 Ari	7 Tau
9 Pis	10 Tau	9 Tau	10 Can	10 Leo	11 Lib	11 Sco	12 Cap	10 Aqu	10 Pis	10 Tau	10 Gem
11 Ari	12 Gem	11 Gem	13 Leo	13 Vir	14 Sco	13 Sag	14 Aqu	12 Pis	12 Ari	12 Gem	12 Can
13 Tau	15 Can	14 Can	15 Vir	15 Lib	16 Sag	15 Cap	16 Pis	14 Ari	14 Tau	15 Can	15 Leo
16 Gem	17 Leo	16 Leo	18 Lib	17 Sco	18 Cap	17 Aqu	18 Ari	16 Tau	16 Gem	17 Leo	17 Vir
18 Can	20 Vir	19 Vir	20 Sco	20 Sag	20 Aqu	19 Pis	20 Tau	19 Gem	18 Can	20 Vir	20 Lib
21 Leo	22 Lib	21 Lib	22 Sag	22 Cap	22 Pis	21 Ari	22 Gem	21 Can	21 Leo	22 Lib	22 Sco
23 Vir	24 Sco	24 Sco	24 Cap	24 Aqu	24 Ari	24 Tau	25 Can	24 Vir	23 Vir	25 Sco	24 Sag
26 Lib	26 Sag	26 Sag	26 Aqu	26 Pis	28 Tau	26 Gem	27 Leo	26 Lib	26 Lib	27 Sag	26 Cap
28 Sco		28 Cap	29 Pis	28 Ari	29 Gem	28 Can	30 Vir	29 Lib	28 Sco	29 Cap	28 Aqu
30 Sag		30 Aqu		30 Tau		31 Leo			30 Sag		30 Pis

59

1944

JAN.	FEB.	MAR.	APR.	MAY	JUN.	JUL.	AUG.	SEP.	OCT.	NOV.	DEC.
2 Ari	2 Gem	1 Gem	2 Leo	1 Vir	3 Sco	2 Sag	1 Cap	2 Pis	1 Ari	2 Gem	1 Can
4 Tau	5 Can	3 Can	4 Vir	4 Lib	5 Sag	5 Cap	3 Aqu	4 Ari	3 Tau	4 Can	3 Leo
6 Gem	7 Leo	5 Leo	7 Lib	6 Sco	7 Cap	7 Aqu	5 Pis	6 Tau	5 Gem	6 Leo	6 Vir
8 Can	10 Vir	8 Vir	9 Sco	9 Sag	9 Aqu	9 Pis	7 Ari	8 Gem	7 Can	9 Vir	8 Lib
11 Leo	12 Lib	10 Lib	11 Sag	11 Cap	12 Pis	11 Ari	9 Tau	10 Can	10 Leo	11 Lib	11 Sco
13 Vir	15 Sco	13 Sco	14 Cap	13 Aqu	14 Ari	13 Tau	11 Gem	12 Leo	12 Vir	14 Sco	13 Sag
16 Lib	17 Sag	15 Sag	16 Aqu	15 Pis	16 Tau	15 Gem	14 Can	15 Vir	15 Lib	16 Sag	16 Cap
18 Sco	19 Cap	18 Cap	18 Pis	17 Ari	18 Gem	18 Can	16 Leo	17 Lib	17 Sco	18 Cap	18 Aqu
21 Sag	21 Aqu	20 Aqu	20 Ari	20 Tau	20 Can	20 Leo	19 Vir	20 Sco	20 Sag	21 Aqu	20 Pis
23 Cap	23 Pis	22 Pis	22 Tau	22 Gem	23 Leo	22 Vir	21 Lib	22 Sag	22 Cap	23 Pis	22 Ari
25 Aqu	25 Ari	24 Ari	24 Gem	24 Can	25 Vir	25 Lib	24 Sco	25 Cap	24 Aqu	25 Ari	24 Tau
27 Pis	27 Tau	26 Tau	27 Can	26 Leo	28 Lib	27 Sco	26 Sag	27 Aqu	26 Pis	27 Tau	26 Gem
29 Ari		28 Gem	29 Leo	29 Vir	30 Sco	30 Sag	29 Cap	29 Pis	29 Ari	29 Gem	29 Can
31 Tau		30 Can		31 Lib			31 Aqu		31 Tau		31 Leo

1945

JAN.	FEB.	MAR.	APR.	MAY	JUN.	JUL.	AUG.	SEP.	OCT.	NOV.	DEC.
2 Vir	1 Lib	3 Sco	2 Sag	1 Cap	2 Pis	2 Ari	2 Gem	3 Leo	2 Vir	1 Lib	1 Sco
5 Lib	4 Sco	5 Sag	4 Cap	4 Aqu	4 Ari	4 Tau	4 Can	5 Vir	5 Lib	3 Sco	3 Sag
7 Sco	6 Sag	8 Cap	6 Aqu	6 Pis	6 Tau	6 Gem	6 Leo	7 Lib	7 Sco	6 Sag	6 Cap
10 Sag	8 Cap	10 Aqu	9 Pis	8 Ari	8 Gem	8 Can	9 Vir	10 Sco	10 Sag	8 Cap	8 Aqu
12 Cap	11 Aqu	12 Pis	11 Ari	10 Tau	10 Can	10 Leo	11 Lib	12 Sag	12 Cap	11 Aqu	10 Pis
14 Aqu	13 Pis	14 Ari	13 Tau	12 Gem	13 Leo	12 Vir	14 Sco	15 Cap	15 Aqu	13 Pis	13 Ari
16 Pis	15 Ari	16 Tau	15 Gem	14 Can	15 Vir	15 Lib	16 Sag	17 Aqu	17 Pis	15 Ari	15 Tau
18 Ari	17 Tau	18 Gem	17 Can	16 Leo	17 Lib	17 Sco	19 Cap	19 Pis	19 Ari	17 Tau	17 Gem
20 Tau	19 Gem	20 Can	19 Leo	19 Vir	20 Sco	20 Sag	21 Aqu	21 Ari	21 Tau	19 Gem	19 Can
23 Gem	21 Can	23 Leo	21 Vir	21 Lib	22 Sag	22 Cap	23 Pis	23 Tau	23 Gem	21 Can	21 Leo
25 Can	23 Leo	25 Vir	24 Lib	24 Sco	25 Cap	25 Aqu	25 Ari	25 Gem	25 Can	23 Leo	23 Vir
27 Leo	26 Vir	28 Lib	26 Sco	26 Sag	27 Aqu	27 Pis	27 Tau	28 Can	27 Leo	26 Vir	25 Lib
30 Vir	28 Lib	30 Sco	29 Sag	29 Cap	29 Pis	29 Ari	29 Gem	30 Leo	29 Vir	28 Lib	28 Sco
				31 Aqu		31 Tau	31 Can				31 Sag

1946

JAN.	FEB.	MAR.	APR.	MAY	JUN.	JUL.	AUG.	SEP.	OCT.	NOV.	DEC.
2 Cap	1 Aqu	2 Pis	1 Ari	2 Gem	1 Can	2 Vir	1 Lib	2 Sag	2 Cap	1 Aqu	1 Pis
4 Aqu	3 Pis	4 Ari	3 Tau	4 Can	3 Leo	5 Lib	3 Sco	5 Cap	5 Aqu	3 Pis	3 Ari
7 Pis	5 Ari	7 Tau	5 Gem	6 Leo	5 Vir	7 Sco	6 Sag	7 Aqu	7 Pis	6 Ari	5 Tau
9 Ari	7 Tau	9 Gem	7 Can	9 Vir	7 Lib	10 Sag	8 Cap	10 Pis	9 Ari	8 Tau	7 Gem
11 Tau	9 Gem	11 Can	9 Leo	11 Lib	10 Sco	12 Cap	11 Aqu	12 Ari	11 Tau	10 Gem	9 Can
13 Gem	12 Can	13 Leo	11 Vir	14 Sco	12 Sag	15 Aqu	13 Pis	14 Tau	13 Gem	12 Can	11 Leo
15 Can	14 Leo	15 Vir	14 Lib	16 Sag	15 Cap	17 Pis	15 Ari	16 Gem	15 Can	14 Leo	13 Vir
17 Leo	16 Vir	18 Lib	16 Sco	19 Cap	17 Aqu	19 Ari	18 Tau	18 Can	18 Leo	16 Vir	16 Lib
20 Vir	18 Lib	20 Sco	19 Sag	21 Aqu	20 Pis	21 Tau	20 Gem	20 Leo	20 Vir	18 Lib	18 Sco
22 Lib	21 Sco	23 Sag	21 Cap	23 Pis	22 Ari	24 Gem	22 Can	23 Vir	22 Lib	21 Sco	20 Sag
24 Sco	23 Sag	25 Cap	24 Aqu	26 Ari	24 Tau	26 Can	24 Leo	25 Lib	24 Sco	23 Sag	23 Cap
27 Sag	26 Cap	27 Aqu	26 Pis	28 Tau	26 Gem	28 Leo	26 Vir	27 Sco	27 Sag	26 Cap	25 Aqu
29 Cap	28 Aqu	30 Pis	28 Ari	30 Gem	28 Can	30 Vir	28 Lib	30 Sag	29 Cap	28 Aqu	28 Pis
			30 Tau		30 Leo		31 Sco				30 Ari

1947

JAN.	FEB.	MAR.	APR.	MAY	JUN.	JUL.	AUG.	SEP.	OCT.	NOV.	DEC.
2 Tau	2 Can	1 Can	2 Vir	1 Lib	2 Sag	2 Cap	1 Aqu	2 Ari	2 Tau	2 Can	2 Leo
4 Gem	4 Leo	3 Leo	4 Lib	4 Sco	5 Cap	5 Aqu	3 Pis	4 Tau	4 Gem	4 Leo	4 Vir
6 Can	6 Vir	6 Vir	6 Sco	6 Sag	7 Aqu	7 Pis	6 Ari	7 Gem	6 Can	6 Vir	6 Lib
8 Leo	8 Lib	8 Lib	9 Sag	8 Cap	10 Pis	10 Ari	8 Tau	9 Can	8 Leo	9 Lib	8 Sco
10 Vir	11 Sco	10 Sco	11 Cap	11 Aqu	12 Ari	12 Tau	10 Gem	11 Leo	10 Vir	11 Sco	10 Sag
12 Lib	13 Sag	12 Sag	14 Aqu	14 Pis	14 Tau	14 Gem	12 Can	13 Vir	12 Lib	13 Sag	13 Cap
14 Sco	16 Cap	15 Cap	16 Pis	16 Ari	17 Gem	16 Can	14 Leo	15 Lib	14 Sco	16 Cap	15 Aqu
17 Sag	18 Aqu	17 Aqu	18 Ari	18 Tau	19 Can	18 Leo	16 Vir	17 Sco	17 Sag	18 Aqu	18 Pis
19 Cap	20 Pis	20 Pis	21 Tau	20 Gem	21 Leo	20 Vir	19 Lib	19 Sag	19 Cap	21 Pis	20 Ari
22 Aqu	23 Ari	22 Ari	23 Gem	22 Can	23 Vir	22 Lib	21 Sco	22 Cap	22 Aqu	23 Ari	23 Tau
24 Pis	25 Tau	24 Tau	25 Can	24 Leo	25 Lib	24 Sco	23 Sag	24 Aqu	24 Pis	25 Tau	25 Gem
27 Ari	27 Gem	26 Gem	27 Leo	26 Vir	27 Sco	27 Sag	26 Cap	27 Pis	27 Ari	27 Gem	27 Can
29 Tau		29 Can	29 Vir	29 Lib	30 Sag	29 Cap	28 Aqu	29 Ari	29 Tau	30 Can	29 Leo
31 Gem		31 Leo		31 Sco			31 Pis		31 Gem		31 Vir

1948

JAN.	FEB.	MAR.	APR.	MAY	JUN.	JUL.	AUG.	SEP.	OCT.	NOV.	DEC.
2 Lib	1 Sco	1 Sag	2 Aqu	2 Pis	1 Ari	1 Tau	2 Can	2 Vir	2 Lib	2 Sag	2 Cap
4 Vir	3 Sag	4 Cap	5 Pis	5 Ari	4 Tau	3 Gem	4 Leo	4 Lib	4 Sco	4 Cap	4 Aqu
7 Sag	5 Cap	6 Aqu	7 Ari	7 Tau	6 Gem	5 Can	6 Vir	6 Sco	6 Sag	7 Aqu	7 Pis
9 Cap	8 Aqu	9 Pis	10 Tau	9 Gem	8 Can	7 Leo	8 Lib	8 Sag	8 Cap	9 Pis	9 Ari
12 Aqu	10 Pis	11 Ari	12 Gem	12 Can	10 Leo	9 Vir	10 Sco	11 Cap	11 Aqu	12 Ari	12 Tau
14 Pis	13 Ari	14 Tau	14 Can	14 Leo	12 Vir	11 Lib	12 Sag	13 Aqu	13 Pis	14 Tau	14 Gem
17 Ari	15 Tau	16 Gem	17 Leo	16 Vir	14 Lib	14 Sco	15 Cap	16 Pis	16 Ari	17 Gem	16 Can
19 Tau	18 Gem	18 Can	19 Vir	18 Lib	16 Sco	16 Sag	17 Aqu	18 Ari	18 Tau	19 Can	18 Leo
21 Gem	20 Can	20 Leo	21 Lib	20 Sco	19 Sag	18 Cap	20 Pis	21 Tau	20 Gem	21 Leo	21 Vir
23 Can	22 Leo	22 Vir	23 Sco	22 Sag	21 Cap	21 Aqu	22 Ari	23 Gem	23 Can	23 Vir	23 Lib
25 Leo	24 Vir	24 Lib	25 Sag	25 Cap	23 Aqu	23 Pis	25 Tau	25 Can	25 Leo	25 Lib	25 Sco
27 Vir	26 Lib	26 Sco	27 Cap	27 Aqu	26 Pis	26 Ari	27 Gem	28 Leo	27 Vir	28 Sco	27 Sag
29 Lib	28 Sco	29 Sag	30 Aqu	30 Pis	28 Ari	28 Tau	29 Can	30 Vir	29 Lib	30 Sag	29 Cap
		31 Cap				31 Gem	31 Leo		31 Sco		

1949

JAN.	FEB.	MAR.	APR.	MAY	JUN.	JUL.	AUG.	SEP.	OCT.	NOV.	DEC.
1 Aqu	2 Ari	1 Ari	2 Gem	2 Can	3 Leo	2 Lib	3 Sag	1 Cap	1 Aqu	2 Ari	2 Tau
3 Pis	4 Tau	4 Tau	5 Can	4 Leo	3 Vir	4 Sco	5 Cap	3 Aqu	3 Pis	4 Tau	4 Gem
6 Ari	7 Gem	6 Gem	7 Leo	6 Vir	5 Lib	6 Sag	7 Aqu	6 Pis	5 Ari	7 Gem	6 Can
8 Tau	9 Can	9 Can	9 Vir	9 Lib	7 Sco	9 Cap	9 Pis	8 Ari	8 Tau	9 Can	9 Leo
10 Gem	11 Leo	11 Leo	11 Lib	11 Sco	9 Sag	11 Aqu	12 Ari	11 Tau	11 Gem	12 Leo	11 Vir
13 Can	13 Vir	13 Vir	13 Sco	13 Sag	11 Cap	13 Pis	14 Tau	13 Gem	13 Can	14 Vir	13 Lib
15 Leo	15 Lib	15 Lib	15 Sag	15 Cap	13 Aqu	16 Ari	17 Gem	16 Can	15 Leo	16 Lib	15 Sco
17 Vir	17 Sco	17 Sco	17 Cap	17 Aqu	16 Pis	18 Tau	19 Can	18 Leo	17 Vir	18 Sco	17 Sag
19 Lib	19 Sag	19 Sag	20 Aqu	19 Pis	18 Ari	21 Gem	22 Leo	20 Vir	20 Lib	20 Sag	19 Cap
21 Sco	22 Cap	21 Cap	22 Pis	22 Ari	21 Tau	23 Can	24 Vir	22 Lib	22 Sco	22 Cap	22 Aqu
23 Sag	24 Aqu	23 Aqu	25 Ari	24 Tau	23 Gem	25 Leo	26 Lib	24 Sco	24 Sag	24 Aqu	24 Pis
26 Cap	27 Pis	26 Pis	27 Tau	27 Gem	26 Can	27 Vir	28 Sco	26 Sag	26 Cap	27 Pis	26 Ari
28 Aqu		28 Ari	30 Gem	29 Can	28 Leo	29 Lib	30 Sag	28 Cap	28 Aqu	29 Ari	29 Tau
30 Pis		31 Tau			30 Vir	31 Sco			30 Pis		31 Gem

1950

JAN.	FEB.	MAR.	APR.	MAY	JUN.	JUL.	AUG.	SEP.	OCT.	NOV.	DEC.
3 Can	1 Leo	1 Leo	2 Lib	1 Sco	1 Cap	1 Aqu	2 Ari	1 Tau	3 Can	2 Leo	1 Vir
5 Leo	4 Vir	3 Vir	4 Sco	3 Sag	3 Aqu	3 Pis	4 Tau	3 Gem	5 Leo	4 Vir	4 Lib
7 Vir	6 Lib	5 Lib	6 Sag	5 Cap	6 Pis	5 Ari	7 Gem	6 Can	8 Vir	6 Lib	6 Sco
9 Lib	8 Sco	7 Sco	8 Cap	7 Aqu	8 Ari	8 Tau	9 Can	8 Leo	10 Lib	8 Sco	8 Sag
12 Sco	10 Sag	9 Sag	10 Aqu	9 Pis	11 Tau	10 Gem	12 Leo	10 Vir	12 Sco	10 Sag	10 Cap
14 Sag	12 Cap	11 Cap	12 Pis	12 Ari	13 Gem	13 Can	14 Vir	12 Lib	14 Sag	12 Cap	12 Aqu
16 Cap	14 Aqu	14 Aqu	15 Ari	14 Tau	16 Can	15 Leo	16 Lib	15 Sco	16 Cap	14 Aqu	14 Pis
18 Aqu	17 Pis	16 Pis	17 Tau	17 Gem	18 Leo	18 Vir	18 Sco	17 Sag	18 Aqu	17 Pis	16 Ari
20 Pis	19 Ari	18 Ari	20 Gem	19 Can	20 Vir	20 Lib	20 Sag	19 Cap	20 Pis	19 Ari	19 Tau
23 Ari	22 Tau	21 Tau	22 Can	22 Leo	22 Lib	22 Sco	22 Cap	21 Aqu	23 Ari	21 Tau	21 Gem
25 Tau	24 Gem	23 Gem	25 Leo	24 Vir	25 Sco	24 Sag	25 Aqu	23 Pis	25 Tau	24 Gem	24 Can
28 Gem	27 Can	26 Can	27 Vir	26 Lib	27 Sag	26 Cap	27 Pis	25 Ari	28 Gem	27 Can	26 Leo
30 Can		28 Leo	29 Lib	28 Sco	29 Cap	28 Aqu	29 Ari	28 Tau	30 Can	29 Leo	29 Vir
		30 Vir		30 Sag		30 Pis		30 Gem			31 Lib

1951

JAN.	FEB.	MAR.	APR.	MAY	JUN.	JUL.	AUG.	SEP.	OCT.	NOV.	DEC.
2 Sco	1 Sag	2 Cap	2 Pis	2 Ari	1 Tau	3 Can	2 Leo	3 Lib	2 Sco	1 Sag	2 Aqu
4 Sag	3 Cap	4 Aqu	5 Ari	4 Tau	3 Gem	5 Leo	4 Vir	5 Sco	4 Sag	3 Cap	4 Pis
6 Cap	5 Aqu	6 Pis	7 Tau	7 Gem	6 Can	8 Vir	6 Lib	7 Sag	7 Cap	5 Aqu	6 Ari
8 Aqu	7 Pis	8 Ari	10 Gem	9 Can	8 Leo	10 Lib	9 Sco	9 Cap	9 Aqu	7 Pis	9 Tau
10 Pis	9 Ari	12 Tau	12 Can	12 Leo	11 Vir	13 Sco	11 Sag	11 Aqu	11 Pis	9 Ari	11 Gem
13 Ari	11 Tau	13 Gem	15 Leo	14 Vir	13 Lib	15 Sag	13 Cap	13 Pis	13 Ari	12 Tau	14 Can
15 Tau	14 Gem	16 Can	17 Vir	17 Lib	15 Sco	17 Cap	15 Aqu	16 Ari	15 Tau	14 Gem	16 Leo
18 Gem	16 Can	18 Leo	19 Lib	19 Sco	17 Sag	19 Aqu	17 Pis	18 Tau	18 Gem	16 Can	19 Vir
20 Can	19 Leo	21 Vir	21 Sco	21 Sag	19 Cap	21 Pis	19 Ari	20 Gem	20 Can	19 Leo	21 Lib
23 Leo	21 Vir	23 Lib	23 Sag	23 Cap	21 Aqu	23 Ari	21 Tau	23 Can	23 Leo	21 Vir	23 Sco
25 Vir	23 Lib	25 Sco	25 Cap	25 Aqu	23 Pis	25 Tau	24 Gem	25 Leo	25 Vir	24 Lib	26 Sag
27 Lib	26 Sco	27 Sag	27 Aqu	27 Pis	25 Ari	28 Gem	26 Can	28 Vir	27 Lib	26 Sco	28 Cap
29 Sco	28 Sag	29 Cap	30 Pis	29 Ari	28 Tau	30 Can	29 Leo	30 Lib	30 Sco	28 Sag	30 Aqu
		31 Aqu			30 Gem		31 Vir			30 Cap	

1952

JAN.	FEB.	MAR.	APR.	MAY	JUN.	JUL.	AUG.	SEP.	OCT.	NOV.	DEC.
1 Pis	1 Tau	2 Gem	1 Can	1 Leo	2 Lib	2 Sco	2 Cap	1 Aqu	2 Ari	1 Tau	3 Can
3 Ari	4 Gem	5 Can	3 Leo	3 Vir	4 Sco	4 Sag	4 Aqu	3 Pis	4 Tau	3 Gem	5 Leo
5 Tau	6 Can	7 Leo	6 Vir	6 Lib	7 Sag	6 Cap	6 Pis	5 Ari	7 Gem	5 Can	8 Vir
7 Gem	9 Leo	10 Vir	8 Lib	8 Sco	9 Cap	8 Aqu	8 Ari	7 Tau	9 Can	8 Leo	10 Lib
10 Can	11 Vir	12 Lib	11 Sco	10 Sag	11 Aqu	10 Pis	11 Tau	10 Gem	11 Leo	10 Vir	13 Sco
12 Leo	14 Lib	14 Sco	13 Sag	12 Cap	13 Pis	12 Ari	13 Gem	12 Can	14 Vir	13 Lib	15 Sag
15 Vir	16 Sco	17 Sag	15 Cap	14 Aqu	15 Ari	14 Tau	15 Can	15 Leo	16 Lib	15 Sco	17 Cap
17 Lib	18 Sag	19 Cap	17 Aqu	16 Pis	17 Tau	17 Gem	18 Leo	17 Vir	19 Sco	17 Sag	19 Aqu
20 Sco	20 Cap	21 Aqu	19 Pis	19 Ari	19 Gem	19 Can	20 Vir	19 Lib	21 Sag	20 Cap	21 Pis
22 Sag	22 Aqu	23 Pis	21 Ari	21 Tau	22 Can	22 Leo	23 Lib	22 Sco	23 Cap	22 Aqu	23 Ari
24 Cap	24 Pis	25 Ari	24 Tau	23 Gem	24 Leo	24 Vir	25 Sco	24 Sag	26 Aqu	24 Pis	25 Tau
26 Aqu	27 Ari	27 Tau	26 Gem	26 Can	27 Vir	27 Lib	28 Sag	26 Cap	28 Pis	26 Ari	28 Gem
28 Pis	29 Tau	29 Gem	28 Can	28 Leo	29 Lib	29 Sco	30 Cap	28 Aqu	30 Ari	28 Tau	30 Can
30 Ari				31 Vir		31 Sag		30 Pis		30 Gem	

1953

JAN.	FEB.	MAR.	APR.	MAY	JUN.	JUL.	AUG.	SEP.	OCT.	NOV.	DEC.
1 Leo	3 Lib	2 Lib	1 Sco	3 Cap	1 Aqu	1 Pis	1 Tau	2 Can	1 Leo	3 Lib	2 Sco
4 Vir	5 Sco	4 Sco	3 Sag	5 Aqu	3 Pis	3 Ari	3 Gem	4 Leo	4 Vir	5 Sco	5 Sag
6 Lib	8 Sag	7 Sag	5 Cap	7 Pis	5 Ari	5 Tau	5 Can	7 Vir	6 Lib	8 Sag	7 Cap
9 Sco	10 Cap	9 Cap	8 Aqu	9 Ari	7 Tau	7 Gem	8 Leo	9 Lib	9 Sco	10 Cap	9 Aqu
11 Sag	12 Aqu	11 Aqu	10 Pis	11 Tau	10 Gem	9 Can	10 Vir	12 Sco	11 Sag	12 Aqu	12 Pis
13 Cap	14 Pis	13 Pis	12 Ari	13 Gem	12 Can	12 Leo	13 Lib	14 Sag	14 Cap	14 Pis	14 Ari
15 Aqu	16 Ari	15 Ari	14 Tau	15 Can	14 Leo	14 Vir	15 Sco	16 Cap	16 Aqu	17 Ari	16 Tau
17 Pis	18 Tau	17 Tau	16 Gem	18 Leo	17 Vir	16 Lib	18 Sag	19 Aqu	18 Pis	19 Tau	18 Gem
19 Ari	20 Gem	19 Gem	18 Can	20 Vir	19 Lib	19 Sco	20 Cap	21 Pis	20 Ari	21 Gem	20 Can
22 Tau	22 Can	22 Can	20 Leo	23 Lib	22 Sco	21 Sag	22 Aqu	23 Ari	22 Tau	23 Can	22 Leo
24 Gem	25 Leo	24 Leo	23 Vir	25 Sco	24 Sag	24 Cap	24 Pis	25 Tau	24 Gem	25 Leo	25 Vir
26 Can	27 Vir	27 Vir	26 Lib	28 Sag	26 Cap	26 Aqu	26 Ari	27 Gem	26 Can	27 Vir	27 Lib
29 Leo		29 Lib	28 Sco	30 Cap	28 Aqu	28 Pis	28 Tau	29 Can	29 Leo	30 Lib	30 Sco
31 Vir			30 Sag			30 Ari	30 Gem		31 Vir		

1954

JAN.	FEB.	MAR.	APR.	MAY	JUN.	JUL.	AUG.	SEP.	OCT.	NOV.	DEC.
1 Sag	2 Aqu	2 Aqu	2 Ari	2 Tau	2 Can	2 Leo	3 Lib	1 Sco	1 Sag	2 Aqu	2 Pis
4 Cap	4 Pis	4 Pis	4 Tau	4 Gem	4 Leo	4 Vir	5 Sco	4 Sag	4 Cap	5 Pis	4 Ari
6 Aqu	6 Ari	6 Ari	6 Gem	6 Can	6 Vir	6 Lib	8 Sag	6 Cap	6 Aqu	7 Ari	6 Tau
8 Pis	8 Tau	8 Tau	8 Can	8 Leo	9 Lib	9 Sco	10 Cap	9 Aqu	8 Pis	9 Tau	8 Gem
10 Ari	11 Gem	10 Gem	11 Leo	10 Vir	12 Sco	11 Sag	12 Aqu	11 Pis	11 Ari	11 Gem	10 Can
12 Tau	13 Can	12 Can	13 Vir	13 Lib	14 Sag	14 Cap	15 Pis	13 Ari	13 Tau	13 Can	12 Leo
14 Gem	15 Leo	14 Leo	15 Lib	15 Sco	16 Cap	16 Aqu	17 Ari	15 Tau	14 Gem	15 Leo	15 Vir
16 Can	17 Vir	17 Vir	18 Sco	18 Sag	19 Aqu	18 Pis	19 Tau	17 Gem	17 Can	17 Vir	17 Lib
19 Leo	20 Lib	19 Lib	20 Sag	20 Cap	21 Pis	21 Ari	21 Gem	19 Can	19 Leo	20 Lib	20 Sco
21 Vir	22 Sco	22 Sco	23 Cap	23 Aqu	23 Ari	23 Tau	23 Can	22 Leo	21 Vir	22 Sco	22 Sag
24 Lib	25 Sag	24 Sag	25 Aqu	25 Pis	25 Tau	25 Gem	25 Leo	24 Vir	24 Lib	25 Sag	25 Cap
26 Sco	27 Cap	27 Cap	28 Pis	27 Ari	27 Gem	27 Can	28 Vir	26 Lib	26 Sco	27 Cap	27 Aqu
29 Sag		29 Aqu	30 Ari	29 Tau	29 Can	29 Leo	30 Lib	29 Sco	29 Sag	30 Aqu	29 Pis
31 Cap		31 Pis		31 Gem		31 Vir			31 Cap		

1955

JAN.	FEB.	MAR.	APR.	MAY	JUN.	JUL.	AUG.	SEP.	OCT.	NOV.	DEC.
1 Ari	1 Gem	2 Can	1 Leo	3 Lib	1 Sco	1 Sag	2 Aqu	1 Pis	1 Ari	1 Gem	1 Can
3 Tau	3 Can	5 Leo	3 Vir	5 Sco	4 Sag	4 Cap	5 Pis	3 Ari	3 Tau	3 Can	3 Leo
5 Gem	5 Leo	7 Vir	5 Lib	8 Sag	6 Cap	6 Aqu	7 Ari	6 Tau	5 Gem	5 Leo	5 Vir
7 Can	7 Vir	9 Lib	8 Sco	10 Cap	9 Aqu	9 Pis	9 Tau	8 Gem	7 Can	8 Vir	7 Lib
9 Leo	10 Lib	12 Sco	10 Sag	13 Aqu	11 Pis	11 Ari	11 Gem	10 Can	9 Leo	10 Lib	10 Sco
11 Vir	12 Sco	14 Sag	13 Cap	15 Pis	14 Ari	13 Tau	14 Can	12 Leo	11 Vir	12 Sco	12 Sag
13 Lib	15 Sag	17 Cap	15 Aqu	17 Ari	16 Tau	15 Gem	16 Leo	14 Vir	14 Lib	15 Sag	15 Cap
16 Sco	17 Cap	19 Aqu	18 Pis	19 Tau	18 Gem	17 Can	18 Vir	16 Lib	16 Sco	17 Cap	17 Aqu
18 Sag	20 Aqu	21 Pis	20 Ari	21 Gem	20 Can	19 Leo	20 Lib	19 Sco	18 Sag	20 Aqu	20 Pis
21 Cap	22 Pis	23 Ari	22 Tau	23 Can	22 Leo	21 Vir	22 Sco	21 Sag	21 Cap	22 Pis	22 Ari
23 Aqu	24 Ari	26 Tau	24 Gem	25 Leo	24 Vir	24 Lib	25 Sag	24 Cap	23 Aqu	25 Ari	24 Tau
26 Pis	26 Tau	28 Gem	26 Can	28 Vir	26 Lib	26 Sco	27 Cap	26 Aqu	26 Pis	27 Tau	26 Gem
28 Ari	28 Gem	30 Can	28 Leo	30 Lib	29 Sco	28 Sag	30 Aqu	29 Pis	28 Ari	29 Gem	28 Can
30 Tau			30 Vir			31 Cap			30 Tau		30 Leo

1956

JAN.	FEB.	MAR.	APR.	MAY	JUN.	JUL.	AUG.	SEP.	OCT.	NOV.	DEC.
1 Vir	2 Sco	3 Sag	2 Cap	2 Aqu	3 Ari	2 Tau	1 Gem	1 Leo	1 Vir	1 Sco	1 Sag
3 Lib	5 Sag	5 Cap	4 Aqu	4 Pis	5 Tau	5 Gem	3 Can	3 Vir	3 Lib	4 Sag	3 Cap
6 Sco	7 Cap	8 Aqu	7 Pis	6 Ari	7 Gem	7 Can	5 Leo	6 Lib	5 Sco	6 Cap	6 Aqu
8 Sag	0 Aqu	10 Pis	9 Ari	9 Tau	9 Can	9 Leo	7 Vir	8 Sco	7 Sag	9 Aqu	8 Pis
11 Cap	2 Pis	13 Ari	11 Tau	11 Gem	11 Leo	11 Vir	9 Lib	10 Sag	10 Cap	11 Pis	11 Ari
13 Aqu	4 Ari	15 Tau	13 Gem	13 Can	13 Vir	13 Lib	11 Sco	12 Cap	12 Aqu	14 Ari	13 Tau
16 Pis	7 Tau	17 Gem	16 Can	15 Leo	15 Lib	15 Sco	14 Sag	15 Aqu	15 Pis	16 Tau	16 Gem
18 Ari	19 Gem	19 Can	18 Leo	17 Vir	18 Sco	17 Sag	16 Cap	17 Pis	17 Ari	18 Gem	18 Can
20 Tau	21 Can	21 Leo	20 Vir	19 Lib	20 Sag	20 Cap	19 Aqu	20 Ari	20 Tau	20 Can	20 Leo
23 Gem	23 Leo	23 Vir	22 Lib	21 Sco	23 Cap	22 Aqu	21 Pis	22 Tau	22 Gem	22 Leo	22 Vir
25 Can	25 Vir	26 Lib	24 Sco	24 Sag	25 Aqu	25 Pis	24 Ari	24 Gem	24 Can	24 Vir	24 Lib
27 Leo	27 Lib	28 Sco	27 Sag	26 Cap	28 Pis	27 Ari	26 Tau	27 Can	26 Leo	27 Lib	26 Sco
29 Vir	29 Sco	30 Sag	29 Cap	29 Aqu	30 Ari	30 Tau	28 Gem	29 Leo	28 Vir	29 Sco	28 Sag
31 Lib				31 Pis			30 Can		30 Lib		31 Cap

1957

JAN.	FEB.	MAR.	APR.	MAY	JUN.	JUL.	AUG.	SEP.	OCT.	NOV.	DEC.
2 Aqu	1 Pis	3 Ari	1 Tau	1 Gem	2 Leo	1 Vir	2 Sco	2 Cap	2 Aqu	1 Pis	1 Ari
5 Pis	4 Ari	5 Tau	4 Gem	3 Can	4 Vir	3 Lib	4 Sag	5 Aqu	5 Pis	3 Ari	3 Tau
7 Ari	6 Tau	8 Gem	6 Can	5 Leo	6 Lib	5 Sco	6 Cap	7 Pis	7 Ari	6 Tau	6 Gem
10 Tau	8 Gem	10 Can	8 Leo	8 Vir	8 Sco	8 Sag	9 Aqu	10 Ari	10 Tau	8 Gem	8 Can
12 Gem	10 Can	12 Leo	10 Vir	10 Lib	10 Sag	10 Cap	11 Pis	12 Tau	12 Gem	11 Can	10 Leo
14 Can	12 Leo	14 Vir	12 Lib	12 Sco	13 Cap	12 Aqu	14 Ari	15 Gem	14 Can	13 Leo	12 Vir
16 Leo	14 Vir	16 Lib	14 Sco	14 Sag	15 Aqu	15 Pis	16 Tau	17 Can	17 Leo	15 Vir	14 Lib
18 Vir	16 Lib	18 Sco	17 Sag	16 Cap	18 Pis	17 Ari	19 Gem	19 Leo	19 Vir	17 Lib	16 Sco
20 Lib	19 Sco	20 Sag	19 Cap	19 Aqu	20 Ari	20 Tau	21 Can	21 Vir	21 Lib	19 Sco	19 Sag
22 Sco	21 Sag	23 Cap	21 Aqu	21 Pis	22 Tau	22 Gem	23 Leo	23 Lib	23 Sco	21 Sag	21 Cap
25 Sag	23 Cap	25 Aqu	24 Pis	24 Ari	25 Gem	24 Can	25 Vir	25 Sco	25 Sag	23 Cap	23 Aqu
27 Cap	26 Aqu	28 Pis	26 Ari	26 Tau	27 Can	26 Leo	27 Lib	27 Sag	27 Cap	26 Aqu	26 Pis
29 Aqu	28 Pis	30 Ari	29 Tau	28 Gem	29 Leo	28 Vir	29 Sco	30 Cap	29 Aqu	28 Pis	28 Ari
				31 Can		30 Lib	31 Sag				31 Tau

1958

JAN.	FEB.	MAR.	APR.	MAY	JUN.	JUL.	AUG.	SEP.	OCT.	NOV.	DEC.
2 Gem	1 Can	2 Leo	1 Vir	2 Sco	1 Sag	2 Aqu	1 Pis	2 Tau	2 Gem	1 Can	3 Vir
4 Can	3 Leo	4 Vir	3 Lib	4 Sag	3 Cap	5 Pis	3 Ari	5 Gem	5 Can	3 Leo	5 Lib
6 Leo	5 Vir	6 Lib	5 Sco	6 Cap	5 Aqu	7 Ari	6 Tau	7 Can	7 Leo	3 Vir	7 Sco
8 Vir	7 Lib	8 Sco	7 Sag	9 Aqu	7 Pis	10 Tau	9 Gem	10 Leo	9 Vir	8 Lib	9 Sag
11 Lib	9 Sco	10 Sag	9 Cap	11 Pis	10 Ari	12 Gem	11 Can	12 Vir	11 Lib	10 Sco	11 Cap
13 Sco	11 Sag	13 Cap	11 Aqu	14 Ari	12 Tau	15 Can	13 Leo	14 Lib	13 Sco	12 Sag	13 Aqu
15 Sag	13 Cap	15 Aqu	14 Pis	16 Tau	15 Gem	17 Leo	15 Vir	16 Sco	15 Sag	14 Cap	15 Pis
17 Cap	16 Aqu	17 Pis	16 Ari	18 Gem	17 Can	19 Vir	17 Lib	18 Sag	17 Cap	16 Aqu	18 Ari
19 Aqu	18 Pis	20 Ari	19 Tau	21 Can	19 Leo	21 Lib	19 Sco	20 Cap	19 Aqu	18 Pis	20 Tau
22 Pis	21 Ari	23 Tau	21 Gem	23 Leo	22 Vir	23 Sco	21 Sag	22 Aqu	22 Pis	21 Ari	23 Gem
24 Ari	23 Tau	25 Gem	24 Can	25 Vir	24 Lib	25 Sag	24 Cap	25 Pis	24 Ari	23 Tau	25 Can
27 Tau	26 Gem	27 Can	26 Leo	28 Lib	26 Sco	27 Cap	26 Aqu	27 Ari	27 Tau	26 Gem	28 Leo
29 Gem	28 Can	30 Leo	28 Vir	30 Sco	28 Sag	30 Aqu	28 Pis	30 Tau	29 Gem	28 Can	30 Vir
			30 Lib		30 Cap		31 Ari			30 Leo	

1959

JAN.	FEB.	MAR.	APR.	MAY	JUN.	JUL.	AUG.	SEP.	OCT.	NOV.	DEC.
1 Lib	2 Sag	1 Sag	1 Aqu	1 Pis	2 Tau	2 Gem	1 Can	2 Vir	1 Lib	2 Sag	1 Cap
3 Sco	4 Cap	3 Cap	4 Pis	3 Ari	5 Gem	5 Can	3 Leo	4 Lib	3 Sco	4 Cap	3 Aqu
5 Sag	6 Aqu	5 Aqu	6 Ari	6 Tau	7 Can	7 Leo	6 Vir	6 Sco	6 Sag	6 Aqu	6 Pis
7 Cap	8 Pis	7 Pis	9 Tau	8 Gem	10 Leo	9 Vir	8 Lib	8 Sag	8 Cap	8 Pis	8 Ari
10 Aqu	11 Ari	10 Ari	11 Gem	11 Can	12 Vir	12 Lib	10 Sco	10 Cap	10 Aqu	11 Ari	11 Tau
12 Pis	13 Tau	12 Tau	14 Can	13 Leo	14 Lib	14 Sco	12 Sag	13 Aqu	12 Pis	13 Tau	13 Gem
14 Ari	16 Gem	15 Gem	16 Leo	16 Vir	16 Sco	16 Sag	14 Cap	15 Pis	14 Ari	16 Gem	15 Can
17 Tau	18 Can	17 Can	18 Vir	18 Lib	18 Sag	18 Cap	16 Aqu	17 Ari	17 Tau	18 Can	18 Leo
19 Gem	20 Leo	20 Leo	21 Lib	20 Sco	20 Cap	20 Aqu	18 Pis	19 Tau	19 Gem	21 Leo	20 Vir
22 Can	23 Vir	22 Vir	23 Sco	22 Sag	22 Aqu	22 Pis	21 Ari	22 Gem	22 Can	23 Vir	23 Lib
24 Leo	25 Lib	24 Lib	25 Sag	24 Cap	25 Pis	24 Ari	23 Tau	24 Can	24 Leo	25 Lib	25 Sco
26 Vir	27 Sco	26 Sco	27 Cap	26 Aqu	27 Ari	27 Tau	26 Gem	27 Leo	27 Vir	27 Sco	27 Sag
28 Lib		28 Sag	29 Aqu	28 Pis	29 Tau	29 Gem	28 Can	29 Vir	29 Lib	29 Sag	29 Cap
31 Sco		30 Cap		31 Ari			31 Leo		31 Sco		31 Aqu

1960

JAN.	FEB.	MAR.	APR.	MAY.	JUN.	JUL.	AUG.	SEP.	OCT.	NOV.	DEC.
2 Pis	1 Ari	1 Tau	3 Can	2 Leo	1 Vir	1 Lib	2 Sag	2 Aqu	1 Pis	2 Tau	2 Gem
4 Ari	3 Tau	4 Gem	5 Leo	5 Vir	4 Lib	3 Sco	4 Cap	4 Pis	4 Ari	4 Gem	4 Can
7 Tau	5 Gem	6 Can	8 Vir	7 Lib	6 Sco	5 Sag	6 Aqu	6 Ari	6 Tau	7 Can	7 Leo
9 Gem	8 Can	9 Leo	10 Lib	9 Sco	8 Sag	7 Cap	8 Pis	8 Tau	8 Gem	9 Leo	9 Vir
12 Can	10 Leo	11 Vir	12 Sco	11 Sag	10 Cap	9 Aqu	10 Ari	11 Gem	11 Can	12 Vir	12 Lib
14 Leo	13 Vir	13 Lib	14 Sag	13 Cap	12 Aqu	11 Pis	12 Tau	13 Can	13 Leo	14 Lib	14 Sco
17 Vir	15 Lib	16 Sco	16 Cap	15 Aqu	14 Pis	13 Ari	14 Gem	16 Leo	16 Vir	17 Sco	16 Sag
19 Lib	17 Sco	18 Sag	18 Aqu	18 Pis	16 Ari	16 Tau	17 Can	18 Vir	18 Lib	19 Sag	18 Cap
21 Sco	19 Sag	20 Cap	20 Pis	20 Ari	18 Tau	18 Gem	19 Leo	21 Lib	20 Sco	21 Cap	20 Aqu
23 Sag	22 Cap	22 Aqu	23 Ari	22 Tau	21 Gem	21 Can	22 Vir	23 Sco	22 Sag	23 Aqu	22 Pis
25 Cap	24 Aqu	24 Pis	25 Tau	25 Gem	23 Can	23 Leo	24 Lib	25 Sag	24 Cap	25 Pis	24 Ari
27 Aqu	26 Pis	26 Ari	27 Gem	27 Can	26 Leo	26 Vir	27 Sco	27 Cap	27 Aqu	27 Ari	27 Tau
29 Pis	28 Ari	29 Tau	30 Can	20 Leo	28 Vir	28 Lib	29 Sag	29 Aqu	29 Pis	29 Tau	29 Gem
		31 Gem				30 Sco	31 Cap		31 Ari		31 Sco

1961

JAN.	FEB.	MAR.	APR.	MAY.	JUN.	JUL.	AUG.	SEP.	OCT.	NOV.	DEC.
1 Can	2 Vir	1 Vir	2 Sco	2 Sag	2 Aqu	2 Pis	2 Tau	1 Gem	3 Leo	2 Vir	2 Lib
3 Leo	4 Lib	4 Lib	4 Sag	4 Cap	4 Pis	4 Ari	4 Gem	3 Can	5 Vir	4 Lib	4 Sco
6 Vir	7 Sco	6 Sco	7 Cap	6 Aqu	6 Ari	6 Tau	7 Can	6 Leo	8 Lib	7 Sco	6 Sag
8 Lib	9 Sag	8 Sag	9 Aqu	8 Pis	9 Tau	8 Gem	9 Leo	8 Vir	10 Sco	9 Sag	9 Cap
10 Sco	11 Cap	10 Cap	11 Pis	10 Ari	11 Gem	11 Can	12 Vir	11 Lib	13 Sag	11 Cap	11 Aqu
13 Sag	13 Aqu	12 Aqu	13 Ari	12 Tau	13 Can	13 Leo	14 Lib	13 Sco	15 Cap	13 Aqu	13 Pis
15 Cap	15 Pis	15 Pis	15 Tau	15 Gem	16 Leo	16 Vir	17 Sco	15 Sag	17 Aqu	16 Pis	15 Ari
17 Aqu	17 Ari	17 Ari	17 Gem	17 Can	18 Vir	18 Lib	19 Sag	18 Cap	19 Pis	18 Ari	17 Tau
19 Pis	19 Tau	19 Tau	20 Can	20 Leo	21 Lib	21 Sco	21 Cap	20 Aqu	21 Ari	20 Tau	19 Gem
21 Ari	22 Gem	21 Gem	22 Leo	22 Vir	23 Sco	23 Sag	23 Aqu	22 Pis	23 Tau	22 Gem	22 Can
23 Tau	24 Can	23 Can	25 Vir	25 Lib	26 Sag	25 Cap	25 Pis	24 Ari	26 Gem	24 Can	24 Leo
25 Gem	27 Leo	26 Leo	27 Lib	27 Sco	28 Cap	27 Aqu	27 Ari	26 Tau	28 Can	27 Leo	26 Vir
28 Can		28 Vir	30 Sco	29 Sag	30 Aqu	29 Pis	30 Tau	28 Gem	30 Leo	29 Vir	29 Lib
30 Leo		31 Lib		31 Cap		31 Ari		30 Can			31 Sco

1962

JAN.	FEB.	MAR.	APR.	MAY	JUN.	JUL.	AUG.	SEP.	OCT.	NOV.	DEC.
3 Sag	1 Cap	1 Cap	1 Pis	1 Ari	1 Gem	1 Can	2 Vir	1 Lib	3 Sag	2 Cap	1 Aqu
5 Cap	3 Aqu	3 Aqu	3 Ari	3 Tau	3 Can	3 Leo	4 Lib	3 Sco	5 Cap	4 Aqu	3 Pis
7 Aqu	5 Pis	5 Pis	5 Tau	5 Gem	6 Leo	6 Vir	7 Sco	6 Sag	8 Aqu	6 Pis	5 Ari
9 Pis	7 Ari	7 Ari	7 Gem	7 Can	8 Vir	8 Lib	9 Sag	8 Cap	10 Pis	8 Ari	8 Tau
11 Ari	10 Tau	9 Tau	10 Can	9 Leo	11 Lib	11 Sco	12 Cap	10 Aqu	12 Ari	10 Tau	10 Gem
13 Tau	12 Gem	11 Gem	12 Leo	12 Vir	13 Sco	13 Sag	14 Aqu	12 Pis	14 Tau	12 Gem	12 Can
16 Gem	14 Can	13 Can	15 Vir	14 Lib	16 Sag	15 Cap	16 Pis	14 Ari	16 Gem	14 Can	14 Leo
18 Can	17 Leo	16 Leo	17 Lib	17 Sco	18 Cap	17 Aqu	18 Ari	16 Tau	18 Can	17 Leo	16 Vir
20 Leo	19 Vir	18 Vir	20 Sco	19 Sag	20 Aqu	19 Pis	20 Tau	18 Gem	20 Leo	19 Vir	19 Lib
23 Vir	22 Lib	21 Lib	22 Sag	22 Cap	22 Pis	22 Ari	22 Gem	21 Can	23 Vir	21 Lib	21 Sco
25 Lib	24 Sco	23 Sco	24 Cap	24 Aqu	24 Ari	24 Tau	24 Can	23 Leo	25 Lib	24 Sco	24 Sag
28 Sco	26 Sag	26 Sag	27 Aqu	26 Pis	26 Tau	26 Gem	27 Leo	25 Vir	28 Sco	26 Sag	26 Cap
30 Sag		28 Cap	29 Pis	28 Ari	29 Gem	28 Can	29 Vir	28 Lib	30 Sag	29 Cap	28 Aqu
		30 Aqu		30 Tau		30 Leo		30 Sco			31 Pis

1963

JAN.	FEB.	MAR.	APR.	MAY	JUN.	JUL.	AUG.	SEP.	OCT.	NOV.	DEC.
2 Ari	2 Gem	1 Gem	2 Leo	2 Vir	1 Lib	3 Sag	2 Cap	3 Pis	2 Ari	1 Tau	2 Can
4 Tau	4 Can	4 Can	5 Vir	4 Lib	3 Sco	5 Cap	4 Aqu	5 Ari	4 Tau	3 Gem	4 Leo
6 Gem	7 Leo	6 Leo	7 Lib	7 Sco	6 Sag	8 Aqu	6 Pis	7 Tau	6 Gem	5 Can	6 Vir
8 Can	9 Vir	8 Vir	10 Sco	9 Sag	8 Cap	10 Pis	8 Ari	9 Gem	8 Can	7 Leo	9 Lib
10 Leo	11 Lib	11 Lib	12 Sag	12 Cap	10 Aqu	12 Ari	10 Tau	11 Can	10 Leo	9 Vir	11 Sco
13 Vir	14 Sco	13 Sco	15 Cap	14 Aqu	13 Pis	14 Tau	13 Gem	13 Leo	13 Vir	11 Lib	14 Sag
15 Lib	16 Sag	16 Sag	17 Aqu	16 Pis	15 Ari	16 Gem	15 Can	15 Vir	15 Lib	14 Sco	16 Cap
18 Sco	19 Cap	18 Cap	19 Pis	19 Ari	17 Tau	18 Can	17 Leo	18 Lib	18 Sco	16 Sag	19 Aqu
20 Sag	21 Aqu	21 Aqu	21 Ari	21 Tau	19 Gem	21 Leo	19 Vir	20 Sco	20 Sag	19 Cap	21 Pis
22 Cap	23 Pis	23 Pis	23 Tau	23 Gem	21 Can	23 Vir	22 Lib	23 Sag	23 Cap	21 Aqu	23 Ari
25 Aqu	25 Ari	25 Ari	25 Gem	25 Can	23 Leo	25 Lib	24 Sco	25 Cap	25 Aqu	24 Pis	25 Tau
27 Pis	27 Tau	27 Tau	27 Can	27 Leo	25 Vir	28 Sco	27 Sag	28 Aqu	27 Pis	26 Ari	27 Gem
29 Ari		29 Gem	29 Leo	29 Vir	28 Lib	30 Sag	29 Cap	30 Pis	30 Ari	28 Tau	29 Can
31 Tau		31 Can			30 Sco		31 Aqu			30 Gem	31 Leo

1964

JAN.	FEB.	MAR.	APR.	MAY	JUN.	JUL.	AUG.	SEP.	OCT.	NOV.	DEC.
3 Vir	1 Lib	2 Sco	1 Sag	1 Cap	2 Pis	2 Ari	2 Gem	1 Can	2 Vir	1 Lib	3 Sag
5 Lib	4 Sco	5 Sag	3 Cap	3 Aqu	4 Ari	4 Tau	4 Can	3 Leo	4 Lib	3 Sco	5 Cap
7 Sco	6 Sag	7 Cap	6 Aqu	6 Pis	6 Tau	6 Gem	6 Leo	5 Vir	7 Sco	5 Sag	8 Aqu
10 Sag	9 Cap	10 Aqu	8 Pis	8 Ari	8 Gem	8 Can	8 Vir	7 Lib	9 Sag	8 Cap	10 Pis
12 Cap	11 Aqu	12 Pis	10 Ari	10 Tau	10 Can	10 Leo	10 Lib	9 Sco	11 Cap	10 Aqu	13 Ari
15 Aqu	13 Pis	14 Ari	13 Tau	12 Gem	12 Leo	12 Vir	13 Sco	12 Sag	14 Aqu	13 Pis	15 Tau
17 Pis	16 Ari	16 Tau	15 Gem	14 Can	15 Vir	14 Lib	15 Sag	14 Cap	16 Pis	15 Ari	17 Gem
19 Ari	18 Tau	18 Gem	17 Can	16 Leo	17 Lib	16 Sco	18 Cap	17 Aqu	19 Ari	17 Tau	19 Can
22 Tau	20 Gem	20 Can	19 Leo	18 Vir	19 Sco	19 Sag	20 Aqu	19 Pis	21 Tau	19 Gem	21 Leo
24 Gem	22 Can	23 Leo	21 Vir	21 Lib	22 Sag	22 Cap	23 Pis	21 Ari	23 Gem	21 Can	23 Vir
26 Can	24 Leo	25 Vir	23 Lib	23 Sco	24 Cap	24 Aqu	25 Ari	23 Tau	25 Can	23 Leo	25 Lib
28 Leo	26 Vir	27 Lib	26 Sco	25 Sag	27 Aqu	26 Pis	27 Tau	26 Gem	27 Leo	26 Vir	27 Sco
30 Vir	29 Lib	29 Sco	28 Sag	28 Cap	29 Pis	29 Ari	29 Gem	28 Can	29 Vir	28 Lib	30 Sag
				30 Aqu		31 Tau		30 Leo		30 Sco	

1965

JAN.	FEB.	MAR.	APR.	MAY	JUN.	JUL.	AUG.	SEP.	OCT.	NOV.	DEC.
1 Cap	3 Pis	2 Pis	1 Ari	2 Gem	1 Can	2 Vir	1 Lib	2 Sag	1 Cap	3 Pis	2 Ari
4 Aqu	5 Ari	4 Ari	3 Tau	4 Can	3 Leo	4 Lib	3 Sco	4 Cap	4 Aqu	5 Ari	5 Tau
6 Pis	7 Tau	7 Tau	5 Gem	7 Leo	5 Vir	7 Sco	5 Sag	6 Aqu	6 Pis	7 Tau	7 Gem
9 Ari	10 Gem	9 Gem	7 Can	9 Vir	7 Lib	9 Sag	8 Cap	9 Pis	9 Ari	10 Gem	9 Can
11 Tau	12 Can	11 Can	9 Leo	11 Lib	9 Sco	11 Cap	10 Aqu	11 Ari	11 Tau	12 Can	11 Leo
13 Gem	14 Leo	13 Leo	11 Vir	13 Sco	12 Sag	14 Aqu	13 Pis	14 Tau	13 Gem	14 Leo	13 Vir
15 Can	16 Vir	15 Vir	14 Lib	15 Sag	14 Cap	16 Pis	15 Ari	16 Gem	16 Can	16 Vir	15 Lib
17 Leo	18 Lib	17 Lib	16 Sco	18 Cap	17 Aqu	19 Ari	18 Tau	18 Can	18 Leo	18 Lib	18 Sco
19 Vir	20 Sco	19 Sco	18 Sag	20 Aqu	19 Pis	21 Tau	20 Gem	20 Leo	20 Vir	20 Sco	20 Sag
21 Lib	22 Sag	22 Sag	21 Cap	23 Pis	22 Ari	24 Gem	22 Can	22 Vir	22 Lib	23 Sag	22 Cap
24 Sco	25 Cap	24 Cap	23 Aqu	25 Ari	24 Tau	26 Can	24 Leo	25 Lib	24 Sco	25 Cap	25 Aqu
26 Sag	27 Aqu	27 Aqu	26 Pis	28 Tau	26 Gem	28 Leo	26 Vir	27 Sco	26 Sag	27 Aqu	27 Pis
29 Cap		29 Pis	28 Ari	30 Gem	28 Can	30 Vir	28 Lib	29 Sag	29 Cap	30 Pis	30 Ari
31 Aqu			30 Tau		30 Leo		30 Sco		31 Aqu		

1966

JAN.	FEB.	MAR.	APR.	MAY	JUN.	JUL.	AUG.	SEP.	OCT.	NOV.	DEC.
1 Tau	2 Can	1 Can	2 Vir	1 Lib	2 Sag	1 Cap	3 Pis	1 Ari	1 Tau	2 Can	2 Leo
4 Gem	4 Leo	4 Leo	4 Lib	3 Sco	4 Cap	4 Aqu	5 Ari	4 Tau	4 Gem	4 Leo	4 Vir
6 Can	6 Vir	6 Vir	6 Sco	6 Sag	7 Aqu	6 Pis	8 Tau	6 Gem	6 Can	7 Vir	6 Lib
8 Leo	8 Lib	7 Lib	8 Sag	8 Cap	9 Pis	9 Ari	10 Gem	9 Can	8 Leo	9 Lib	8 Sco
10 Vir	10 Sco	10 Sco	10 Cap	10 Aqu	12 Ari	11 Tau	12 Can	11 Leo	10 Vir	11 Sco	10 Sag
12 Lib	12 Sag	12 Sag	13 Aqu	13 Pis	14 Tau	14 Gem	14 Leo	13 Vir	12 Lib	13 Sag	12 Cap
14 Sco	15 Cap	14 Cap	15 Pis	15 Ari	16 Gem	16 Can	16 Vir	15 Lib	14 Sco	15 Cap	15 Aqu
16 Sag	17 Aqu	17 Aqu	18 Ari	18 Tau	19 Can	18 Leo	18 Lib	17 Sco	16 Sag	17 Aqu	17 Pis
19 Cap	20 Pis	19 Pis	20 Tau	20 Gem	21 Leo	20 Vir	20 Sco	19 Sag	19 Cap	20 Pis	20 Ari
21 Aqu	22 Ari	22 Ari	23 Gem	22 Can	23 Vir	22 Lib	23 Sag	21 Cap	21 Aqu	22 Ari	22 Tau
24 Pis	25 Tau	24 Tau	25 Can	24 Leo	25 Lib	24 Sco	25 Cap	24 Aqu	23 Pis	25 Tau	25 Gem
26 Ari	27 Gem	26 Gem	27 Leo	26 Vir	27 Sco	26 Sag	27 Aqu	26 Pis	26 Ari	27 Gem	27 Can
29 Tau		29 Can	29 Vir	29 Lib	29 Sag	29 Cap	30 Pis	29 Ari	28 Tau	29 Can	29 Leo
31 Gem		31 Leo		31 Sco		31 Aqu			31 Gem		31 Vir

1967

JAN.	FEB.	MAR.	APR.	MAY	JUN.	JUL.	AUG.	SEP.	OCT.	NOV.	DEC.
2 Lib	1 Sco	2 Sag	1 Cap	3 Pis	1 Ari	1 Tau	2 Can	1 Leo	1 Vir	1 Sco	1 Sag
4 Sco	3 Sag	4 Cap	3 Aqu	5 Ari	4 Tau	4 Gem	5 Leo	3 Vir	3 Lib	3 Sag	3 Cap
7 Sag	5 Cap	7 Aqu	5 Pis	8 Tau	6 Gem	6 Can	7 Vir	5 Lib	5 Sco	5 Cap	5 Aqu
9 Cap	7 Aqu	9 Pis	8 Ari	10 Gem	9 Can	8 Leo	9 Lib	7 Sco	7 Sag	7 Aqu	7 Pis
11 Aqu	10 Pis	12 Ari	10 Tau	12 Can	11 Leo	11 Vir	11 Sco	9 Sag	9 Cap	10 Pis	9 Ari
13 Pis	12 Ari	14 Tau	13 Gem	15 Leo	13 Vir	13 Lib	13 Sag	12 Cap	11 Aqu	12 Ari	12 Tau
16 Ari	15 Tau	17 Gem	15 Can	17 Vir	15 Lib	15 Sco	15 Cap	14 Aqu	13 Pis	15 Tau	14 Gem
18 Tau	17 Gem	19 Can	18 Leo	19 Lib	18 Sco	17 Sag	18 Aqu	16 Pis	16 Ari	17 Gem	17 Can
21 Gem	20 Can	21 Leo	20 Vir	21 Sco	20 Sag	19 Cap	20 Pis	19 Ari	18 Tau	20 Can	19 Leo
23 Can	22 Leo	23 Vir	22 Lib	23 Sag	22 Cap	21 Aqu	22 Ari	21 Tau	21 Gem	22 Leo	22 Vir
25 Leo	24 Vir	25 Lib	24 Sco	25 Cap	24 Aqu	24 Pis	25 Tau	24 Gem	23 Can	24 Vir	24 Lib
27 Vir	26 Lib	27 Sco	26 Sag	27 Aqu	26 Pis	26 Ari	27 Gem	26 Can	26 Leo	27 Lib	26 Sco
30 Lib	28 Sco	29 Sag	28 Cap	30 Pis	29 Ari	29 Tau	30 Can	28 Leo	28 Vir	29 Sco	28 Sag
			30 Aqu			31 Gem			30 Lib		30 Cap

1968

JAN.	FEB.	MAR.	APR.	MAY	JUN.	JUL.	AUG.	SEP.	OCT.	NOV.	DEC.
1 Aqu	2 Ari	3 Tau	2 Gem	2 Can	3 Vir	2 Lib	1 Sco	1 Cap	3 Pis	1 Ari	1 Tau
3 Pis	5 Tau	5 Gem	4 Can	4 Leo	5 Lib	4 Sco	3 Sag	3 Aqu	5 Ari	4 Tau	3 Gem
6 Ari	7 Gem	8 Can	7 Leo	6 Vir	7 Sco	6 Sag	5 Cap	5 Pis	7 Tau	6 Gem	6 Can
8 Tau	10 Can	10 Leo	9 Vir	9 Lib	9 Sag	8 Cap	7 Aqu	8 Ari	10 Gem	9 Can	8 Leo
11 Gem	12 Leo	13 Vir	11 Lib	11 Sco	11 Cap	10 Aqu	9 Pis	10 Tau	12 Can	11 Leo	11 Vir
13 Can	14 Vir	15 Lib	13 Sco	13 Sag	13 Aqu	13 Pis	11 Ari	12 Gem	15 Leo	14 Vir	13 Lib
16 Leo	16 Lib	17 Sco	15 Sag	15 Cap	15 Pis	15 Ari	14 Tau	15 Can	17 Vir	16 Lib	15 Sco
18 Vir	18 Sco	19 Sag	17 Cap	17 Aqu	18 Ari	17 Tau	16 Gem	17 Leo	19 Lib	18 Sco	17 Sag
20 Lib	21 Sag	21 Cap	19 Aqu	19 Pis	20 Tau	20 Gem	19 Can	20 Vir	22 Sco	20 Sag	19 Cap
22 Sco	23 Cap	23 Aqu	22 Pis	21 Ari	23 Gem	22 Can	21 Leo	22 Lib	24 Sag	22 Cap	21 Aqu
24 Sag	25 Aqu	25 Pis	24 Ari	24 Tau	25 Can	25 Leo	24 Vir	24 Sco	26 Cap	24 Aqu	23 Pis
26 Cap	27 Pis	28 Ari	27 Tau	26 Gem	28 Leo	27 Vir	26 Lib	26 Sag	28 Aqu	26 Pis	26 Ari
29 Aqu	29 Ari	30 Tau	29 Gem	29 Can	30 Vir	29 Lib	28 Sco	28 Cap	30 Pis	28 Ari	28 Tau
31 Pis				31 Leo			30 Sag	30 Aqu			31 Gem

1969

JAN.	FEB.	MAR.	APR.	MAY	JUN.	JUL.	AUG.	SEP.	OCT.	NOV.	DEC.
2 Can	1 Leo	3 Vir	1 Lib	1 Sco	1 Cap	1 Aqu	1 Ari	2 Gem	2 Can	1 Leo	1 Vir
5 Leo	3 Vir	5 Lib	4 Sco	3 Sag	3 Aqu	3 Pis	4 Tau	5 Can	5 Leo	4 Vir	3 Lib
7 Vir	6 Lib	7 Sco	6 Sag	5 Cap	5 Pis	5 Ari	6 Gem	7 Leo	7 Vir	6 Lib	6 Sco
9 Lib	8 Sco	9 Sag	8 Cap	7 Aqu	8 Ari	7 Tau	9 Can	10 Vir	10 Lib	8 Sco	8 Sag
12 Sco	10 Sag	11 Cap	10 Aqu	9 Pis	10 Tau	10 Gem	11 Leo	12 Lib	12 Sco	10 Sag	10 Cap
14 Sag	12 Cap	14 Aqu	12 Pis	11 Ari	13 Gem	12 Can	14 Vir	15 Sco	14 Sag	12 Cap	12 Aqu
16 Cap	14 Aqu	16 Pis	14 Ari	14 Tau	15 Can	15 Leo	16 Lib	17 Sag	16 Cap	14 Aqu	14 Pis
18 Aqu	16 Pis	18 Ari	17 Tau	16 Gem	18 Leo	17 Vir	18 Sco	19 Cap	18 Aqu	17 Pis	16 Ari
20 Pis	18 Ari	20 Tau	19 Gem	19 Can	20 Vir	20 Lib	20 Sag	21 Aqu	20 Pis	19 Ari	18 Tau
22 Ari	21 Tau	23 Gem	21 Can	21 Leo	22 Lib	22 Sco	23 Cap	23 Pis	22 Ari	21 Tau	20 Gem
24 Tau	23 Gem	25 Can	24 Leo	24 Vir	25 Sco	24 Sag	25 Aqu	25 Ari	25 Tau	23 Gem	23 Can
27 Gem	26 Can	28 Leo	26 Vir	26 Lib	27 Sag	26 Cap	27 Pis	27 Tau	27 Gem	26 Can	26 Leo
29 Can	28 Leo	30 Vir	29 Lib	28 Sco	29 Cap	28 Aqu	29 Ari	30 Gem	30 Can	28 Leo	28 Vir
				30 Sag		30 Pis	31 Tau				31 Lib

1970

JAN.	FEB.	MAR.	APR.	MAY	JUN.	JUL.	AUG.	SEP.	OCT.	NOV.	DEC.
2 Sco	1 Sag	2 Cap	3 Pis	2 Ari	3 Gem	2 Can	1 Leo	2 Lib	2 Sco	1 Sag	2 Aqu
4 Sag	3 Cap	4 Aqu	5 Ari	4 Tau	5 Can	5 Leo	3 Vir	5 Sco	4 Sag	3 Cap	4 Pis
6 Cap	5 Aqu	6 Pis	7 Tau	6 Gem	7 Leo	7 Vir	6 Lib	7 Sag	7 Cap	5 Aqu	7 Ari
8 Aqu	7 Pis	8 Ari	9 Gem	9 Can	10 Vir	10 Lib	8 Sco	9 Cap	9 Aqu	7 Pis	9 Tau
10 Pis	9 Ari	10 Tau	11 Can	11 Leo	12 Lib	12 Sco	11 Sag	12 Aqu	11 Pis	9 Ari	11 Gem
12 Ari	11 Tau	12 Gem	14 Leo	14 Vir	15 Sco	14 Sag	13 Cap	14 Pis	13 Ari	11 Tau	13 Can
15 Tau	13 Gem	15 Can	16 Vir	16 Lib	17 Sag	17 Cap	15 Aqu	15 Ari	15 Tau	14 Gem	15 Leo
17 Gem	16 Can	17 Leo	19 Lib	18 Sco	19 Cap	19 Aqu	17 Pis	18 Tau	17 Gem	16 Can	18 Vir
19 Can	18 Leo	20 Vir	21 Sco	21 Sag	21 Aqu	21 Pis	19 Ari	20 Gem	19 Can	18 Leo	20 Lib
22 Leo	21 Vir	22 Lib	23 Sag	23 Cap	23 Pis	23 Ari	21 Tau	22 Can	22 Leo	21 Vir	23 Sco
24 Vir	23 Lib	25 Sco	26 Cap	25 Aqu	25 Ari	25 Tau	23 Gem	24 Leo	24 Vir	23 Lib	25 Sag
27 Lib	26 Sco	27 Sag	28 Aqu	27 Pis	28 Tau	27 Gem	26 Can	27 Vir	27 Lib	26 Sco	28 Cap
29 Sco	28 Sag	29 Cap	30 Pis	29 Ari	30 Gem	29 Can	28 Leo	30 Lib	29 Sco	28 Sag	30 Aqu
		31 Aqu		31 Tau			31 Vir			30 Cap	

1971

JAN.	FEB.	MAR.	APR.	MAY	JUN.	JUL.	AUG.	SEP.	OCT.	NOV.	DEC.
1 Pis	1 Tau	1 Tau	1 Can	1 Leo	2 Lib	2 Sco	1 Sag	2 Aqu	1 Pis	2 Tau	1 Gem
3 Ari	3 Gem	3 Gem	4 Leo	3 Vir	5 Sco	5 Sag	3 Cap	4 Pis	3 Ari	4 Gem	3 Can
5 Tau	6 Can	5 Can	6 Vir	6 Lib	7 Sag	7 Cap	5 Aqu	6 Ari	5 Tau	6 Can	5 Leo
7 Gem	8 Leo	7 Leo	8 Lib	8 Sco	9 Cap	9 Aqu	7 Pis	8 Tau	7 Gem	8 Leo	8 Vir
9 Can	11 Vir	10 Vir	11 Sco	11 Sag	12 Aqu	11 Pis	9 Ari	10 Gem	9 Can	10 Vir	10 Lib
12 Leo	13 Lib	12 Lib	14 Sag	13 Cap	14 Pis	13 Ari	12 Tau	12 Can	12 Leo	13 Lib	13 Sco
14 Vir	16 Sco	15 Sco	16 Cap	15 Aqu	16 Ari	15 Tau	14 Gem	15 Leo	14 Vir	15 Sco	15 Sag
17 Lib	18 Sag	17 Sag	18 Aqu	18 Pis	18 Tau	17 Gem	16 Can	17 Vir	17 Lib	18 Sag	18 Cap
19 Sco	20 Cap	20 Cap	20 Pis	20 Ari	20 Gem	20 Can	18 Leo	19 Lib	19 Sco	20 Cap	20 Aqu
22 Sag	22 Aqu	22 Aqu	22 Ari	22 Tau	22 Can	22 Leo	21 Vir	22 Sco	22 Sag	23 Aqu	22 Pis
24 Cap	24 Pis	24 Pis	24 Tau	24 Gem	25 Leo	24 Vir	23 Lib	24 Sag	24 Cap	25 Pis	24 Ari
26 Aqu	26 Ari	26 Ari	26 Gem	26 Can	27 Vir	27 Lib	26 Sco	27 Cap	27 Aqu	27 Ari	26 Tau
28 Pis		28 Tau	29 Can	28 Leo	30 Lib	29 Sco	28 Sag	29 Aqu	29 Pis	29 Tau	29 Gem
30 Ari		30 Gem		31 Vir			31 Cap		31 Ari		31 Can

73

1972

JAN.	FEB.	MAR.	APR.	MAY	JUN.	JUL.	AUG.	SEP.	OCT.	NOV.	DEC.
2 Leo	1 Vir	1 Lib	3 Sag	2 Cap	1 Aqu	1 Pis	1 Tau	2 Can	1 Leo	2 Lib	2 Sco
4 Vir	3 Lib	4 Sco	5 Cap	5 Aqu	3 Pis	3 Ari	3 Gem	4 Leo	3 Vir	4 Sco	4 Sag
7 Lib	5 Sco	6 Sag	7 Aqu	7 Pis	6 Ari	5 Tau	5 Can	6 Vir	6 Lib	7 Sag	7 Cap
9 Sco	8 Sag	9 Cap	10 Pis	9 Ari	8 Tau	7 Gem	8 Leo	8 Lib	8 Sco	9 Cap	9 Aqu
12 Sag	10 Cap	11 Aqu	12 Ari	11 Tau	10 Gem	9 Can	10 Vir	11 Sco	11 Sag	12 Aqu	12 Pis
14 Cap	13 Aqu	13 Pis	14 Tau	13 Gem	12 Can	11 Leo	12 Lib	13 Sag	13 Cap	14 Pis	14 Ari
16 Aqu	15 Pis	15 Ari	16 Gem	15 Can	14 Leo	13 Vir	15 Sco	16 Cap	16 Aqu	17 Ari	16 Tau
18 Pis	17 Ari	17 Tau	18 Can	17 Leo	16 Vir	16 Lib	17 Sag	18 Aqu	18 Pis	19 Tau	18 Gem
21 Ari	19 Tau	19 Gem	20 Leo	20 Vir	18 Lib	18 Sco	20 Cap	21 Pis	20 Ari	21 Gem	20 Can
23 Tau	21 Gem	21 Can	22 Vir	22 Lib	21 Sco	21 Sag	22 Aqu	23 Ari	22 Tau	23 Can	22 Leo
25 Gem	23 Can	24 Leo	25 Lib	25 Sco	23 Sag	23 Cap	24 Pis	25 Tau	24 Gem	25 Leo	24 Vir
27 Can	26 Leo	26 Vir	27 Sco	27 Sag	26 Cap	26 Aqu	26 Ari	27 Gem	26 Can	27 Vir	26 Lib
29 Leo	28 Vir	29 Lib	30 Sag	30 Cap	28 Aqu	28 Pis	28 Tau	29 Can	28 Leo	29 Lib	29 Sco
		31 Sco				30 Ari	30 Gem		31 Vir		31 Sag

1973

JAN.	FEB.	MAR.	APR.	MAY	JUN.	JUL.	AUG.	SEP.	OCT.	NOV.	DEC.
3 Cap	2 Aqu	1 Aqu	2 Ari	2 Tau	2 Can	1 Leo	2 Lib	1 Sco	3 Cap	2 Aqu	2 Pis
5 Aqu	4 Pis	3 Pis	4 Tau	4 Gem	4 Leo	3 Vir	4 Sco	3 Sag	6 Aqu	4 Pis	4 Ari
8 Pis	6 Ari	6 Ari	6 Gem	6 Can	6 Vir	6 Lib	7 Sag	6 Cap	8 Pis	7 Ari	6 Tau
10 Ari	9 Tau	8 Tau	8 Can	8 Leo	8 Lib	8 Sco	9 Cap	8 Aqu	10 Ari	9 Tau	8 Gem
12 Tau	11 Gem	10 Gem	10 Leo	10 Vir	11 Sco	11 Sag	12 Aqu	11 Pis	12 Tau	11 Gem	10 Can
14 Gem	13 Can	12 Can	13 Vir	12 Lib	13 Sag	13 Cap	14 Pis	13 Ari	15 Gem	13 Can	12 Leo
16 Can	15 Leo	14 Leo	15 Lib	15 Sco	16 Cap	16 Aqu	17 Ari	15 Tau	17 Can	15 Leo	14 Vir
18 Leo	17 Vir	16 Vir	17 Sco	17 Sag	18 Aqu	18 Pis	19 Tau	17 Gem	19 Leo	17 Vir	17 Lib
21 Vir	19 Lib	19 Lib	20 Sag	20 Cap	21 Pis	20 Ari	21 Gem	19 Can	21 Vir	19 Lib	19 Sco
23 Lib	22 Sco	21 Sco	22 Cap	22 Aqu	23 Ari	23 Tau	23 Can	22 Leo	23 Lib	22 Sco	21 Sag
25 Sco	24 Sag	23 Sag	25 Aqu	25 Pis	25 Tau	25 Gem	25 Leo	24 Vir	25 Sco	24 Sag	24 Cap
28 Sag	27 Cap	26 Cap	27 Pis	27 Ari	27 Gem	27 Can	27 Vir	26 Lib	28 Sag	27 Cap	26 Aqu
30 Cap		28 Aqu	29 Ari	29 Tau	29 Can	29 Leo	29 Lib	28 Sco	30 Cap	29 Aqu	29 Pis
		31 Pis		31 Gem		31 Vir		30 Sag			31 Ari

1974

JAN.	FEB.	MAR.	APR.	MAY	JUN.	JUL.	AUG.	SEP.	OCT.	NOV.	DEC.
3 Tau	1 Gem	3 Can	1 Leo	2 Lib	1 Sco	1 Sag	2 Aqu	1 Pis	3 Tau	1 Gem	1 Can
5 Gem	3 Can	5 Leo	3 Vir	5 Sco	3 Sag	3 Can	4 Pis	3 Ari	5 Gem	3 Can	3 Leo
7 Can	5 Leo	7 Vir	5 Lib	7 Sag	6 Cap	6 Aqu	7 Ari	5 Tau	7 Can	6 Leo	5 Vir
9 Leo	7 Vir	9 Lib	7 Sco	9 Cap	8 Aqu	8 Pis	9 Tau	8 Gem	9 Leo	8 Vir	7 Lib
11 Vir	9 Lib	11 Sco	10 Sag	12 Aqu	11 Pis	11 Ari	12 Gem	10 Can	11 Vir	10 Lib	9 Sco
13 Lib	12 Sco	13 Sag	12 Cap	14 Pis	13 Ari	13 Tau	14 Can	12 Leo	14 Lib	12 Sco	12 Sag
15 Sco	14 Sag	16 Cap	15 Aqu	17 Ari	16 Tau	15 Gem	16 Leo	14 Vir	16 Sco	14 Sag	14 Cap
18 Sag	16 Cap	18 Aqu	17 Pis	19 Tau	18 Gem	17 Can	18 Vir	16 Lib	18 Sag	17 Cap	16 Aqu
20 Cap	19 Aqu	21 Pis	20 Ari	21 Gem	20 Can	19 Leo	20 Lib	18 Sco	20 Cap	19 Aqu	19 Pis
23 Aqu	21 Pis	23 Ari	22 Tau	23 Can	22 Leo	21 Vir	22 Sco	20 Sag	23 Aqu	22 Pis	21 Ari
25 Pis	24 Ari	25 Tau	24 Gem	25 Leo	24 Vir	23 Lib	24 Sag	23 Cap	25 Pis	24 Ari	24 Tau
28 Ari	26 Tau	28 Gem	26 Can	28 Vir	26 Lib	25 Sco	27 Cap	25 Aqu	28 Ari	26 Tau	26 Gem
30 Tau	28 Gem	30 Can	28 Leo	30 Lib	28 Sco	28 Sag	29 Aqu	28 Pis	30 Tau	29 Gem	28 Can
			30 Vir			30 Cap		30 Ari			30 Leo

1975

JAN.	FEB.	MAR.	APR.	MAY	JUN.	JUL.	AUG.	SEP.	OCT.	NOV.	DEC.
1 Vir	2 Sco	1 Sco	2 Cap	2 Aqu	1 Pis	3 Tau	2 Gem	2 Leo	2 Vir	2 Sco	2 Sag
3 Lib	4 Sag	3 Sag	4 Aqu	4 Pis	3 Ari	5 Gem	4 Can	4 Vir	4 Lib	4 Sag	4 Cap
6 Sco	6 Cap	6 Cap	7 Pis	7 Ari	6 Tau	8 Can	6 Leo	6 Lib	6 Sco	7 Cap	6 Aqu
8 Sag	9 Aqu	8 Aqu	9 Ari	9 Tau	8 Gem	10 Leo	8 Vir	8 Sco	8 Sag	9 Aqu	9 Pis
10 Cap	11 Pis	11 Pis	12 Tau	12 Gem	10 Can	12 Vir	10 Lib	11 Sag	10 Cap	11 Pis	11 Ari
13 Aqu	14 Ari	13 Ari	14 Gem	14 Can	12 Leo	14 Lib	12 Sco	13 Cap	13 Aqu	14 Ari	14 Tau
15 Pis	16 Tau	16 Tau	17 Can	16 Leo	14 Vir	16 Sco	14 Sag	15 Aqu	15 Pis	16 Tau	16 Gem
18 Ari	19 Gem	18 Gem	19 Leo	18 Vir	17 Lib	18 Sag	17 Cap	18 Pis	18 Ari	19 Gem	18 Can
20 Tau	21 Can	20 Can	21 Vir	20 Lib	19 Sco	20 Cap	19 Aqu	20 Ari	20 Tau	21 Can	21 Leo
22 Gem	23 Leo	23 Leo	23 Lib	22 Sco	21 Sag	23 Aqu	21 Pis	23 Tau	22 Gem	23 Leo	23 Vir
25 Can	25 Vir	25 Vir	25 Sco	25 Sag	23 Cap	25 Pis	24 Ari	25 Gem	25 Can	26 Vir	25 Lib
27 Leo	27 Lib	27 Lib	27 Sag	27 Cap	25 Aqu	28 Ari	27 Tau	28 Can	27 Leo	20 Lib	27 Sco
29 Vir		29 Sco	29 Cap	29 Aqu	28 Pis	30 Tau	29 Gem	30 Leo	29 Vir	30 Sco	29 Sag
31 Lib		31 Sag			30 Ari		31 Can		31 Lib		31 Cap

75

1976

JAN.	FEB.	MAR.	APR.	MAY	JUN.	JUL.	AUG.	SEP.	OCT.	NOV.	DEC.
3 Aqu	1 Pis	2 Ari	1 Tau	1 Gem	2 Leo	1 Vir	2 Sco	2 Cap	2 Aqu	3 Ari	2 Tau
5 Pis	4 Ari	5 Tau	3 Gem	3 Can	4 Vir	3 Lib	4 Sag	4 Aqu	4 Pis	5 Tau	5 Gem
7 Ari	6 Tau	7 Gem	6 Can	5 Leo	6 Lib	5 Sco	6 Cap	7 Pis	6 Ari	8 Gem	8 Can
10 Tau	9 Gem	10 Can	8 Leo	8 Vir	8 Sco	8 Sag	8 Aqu	9 Ari	9 Tau	10 Can	10 Leo
12 Gem	11 Can	12 Leo	10 Vir	10 Lib	10 Sag	10 Cap	10 Pis	12 Tau	11 Gem	13 Leo	12 Vir
15 Can	13 Leo	14 Vir	12 Lib	12 Sco	12 Cap	12 Aqu	13 Ari	14 Gem	14 Can	15 Vir	14 Lib
17 Leo	15 Vir	17 Lib	14 Sco	14 Sag	14 Aqu	14 Pis	15 Tau	17 Can	16 Leo	17 Lib	17 Sco
19 Vir	17 Lib	18 Sco	16 Sag	16 Cap	17 Pis	17 Ari	18 Gem	19 Leo	19 Vir	19 Sco	19 Sag
21 Lib	20 Sco	20 Sag	18 Cap	18 Aqu	19 Ari	19 Tau	20 Can	21 Vir	21 Lib	21 Sag	21 Cap
23 Sco	22 Sag	22 Cap	21 Aqu	20 Pis	22 Tau	22 Gem	23 Leo	23 Lib	23 Sco	23 Cap	23 Aqu
25 Sag	24 Cap	24 Aqu	23 Pis	23 Ari	24 Gem	24 Can	25 Vir	25 Sco	25 Sag	25 Aqu	25 Pis
28 Cap	26 Aqu	27 Pis	26 Ari	25 Tau	26 Can	26 Leo	27 Lib	27 Sag	27 Cap	28 Pis	27 Ari
30 Aqu	29 Pis	29 Ari	28 Tau	28 Gem	29 Leo	28 Vir	29 Sco	29 Cap	29 Aqu	30 Ari	30 Tau
				30 Can		31 Lib	31 Sag		31 Pis		

1977

JAN.	FEB.	MAR.	APR.	MAY	JUN.	JUL.	AUG.	SEP.	OCT.	NOV.	DEC.
1 Gem	3 Leo	2 Leo	1 Vir	2 Sco	1 Sag	2 Aqu	1 Pis	2 Tau	1 Gem	3 Leo	2 Vir
4 Can	5 Vir	4 Vir	3 Lib	4 Sag	3 Cap	4 Pis	3 Ari	4 Gem	4 Can	5 Vir	5 Lib
6 Leo	7 Lib	6 Lib	5 Sco	6 Cap	5 Aqu	6 Ari	5 Tau	7 Can	6 Leo	7 Lib	7 Sco
8 Vir	9 Sco	8 Sco	7 Sag	8 Aqu	7 Pis	9 Tau	8 Gem	9 Leo	9 Vir	10 Sco	9 Sag
11 Lib	11 Sag	10 Sag	9 Cap	10 Pis	9 Ari	11 Gem	10 Can	11 Vir	11 Lib	12 Sag	11 Cap
13 Sco	13 Cap	13 Cap	11 Aqu	13 Ari	12 Tau	14 Can	13 Leo	14 Lib	13 Sco	14 Cap	13 Aqu
15 Sag	15 Aqu	15 Aqu	13 Pis	15 Tau	14 Gem	16 Leo	15 Vir	16 Sco	15 Sag	16 Aqu	15 Pis
17 Cap	18 Pis	17 Pis	16 Ari	18 Gem	17 Can	19 Vir	17 Lib	18 Sag	17 Cap	18 Pis	17 Ari
19 Aqu	20 Ari	19 Ari	18 Tau	20 Can	19 Leo	21 Lib	19 Sco	20 Cap	19 Aqu	20 Ari	20 Tau
21 Pis	22 Tau	22 Tau	21 Gem	23 Leo	22 Vir	23 Sco	22 Sag	22 Aqu	22 Pis	22 Tau	22 Gem
24 Ari	25 Gem	24 Gem	23 Can	25 Vir	24 Lib	25 Sag	24 Cap	24 Pis	24 Ari	25 Gem	25 Can
26 Tau	27 Can	27 Can	26 Leo	28 Lib	26 Sco	27 Cap	26 Aqu	27 Ari	26 Tau	27 Can	27 Leo
29 Gem		29 Leo	28 Vir	30 Sco	28 Sag	29 Aqu	28 Pis	29 Tau	29 Gem	30 Leo	30 Vir
31 Can			30 Lib		30 Cap		30 Ari		31 Can		

76

1968

JAN.	FEB.	MAR.	APR.	MAY	JUN.	JUL.	AUG.	SEP.	OCT.	NOV.	DEC.
1 Lib	2 Sag	1 Sag	2 Aqu	1 Pis	2 Tau	1 Gem	3 Leo	1 Vir	1 Lib	2 Sag	1 Cap
3 Sco	4 Cap	3 Cap	4 Pis	3 Ari	4 Gem	4 Can	5 Vir	4 Lib	3 Sco	4 Cap	3 Aqu
5 Sag	6 Aqu	5 Aqu	6 Ari	5 Tau	7 Can	6 Leo	8 Lib	6 Sco	6 Sag	6 Aqu	5 Pis
7 Cap	8 Pis	7 Pis	8 Tau	8 Gem	9 Leo	9 Vir	10 Sco	8 Sag	8 Cap	8 Pis	8 Ari
9 Aqu	10 Ari	9 Ari	10 Gem	10 Can	12 Vir	11 Lib	12 Sag	11 Cap	10 Aqu	10 Ari	10 Tau
11 Pis	12 Tau	12 Tau	13 Can	13 Leo	14 Lib	14 Sco	14 Cap	13 Aqu	12 Pis	13 Tau	12 Gem
14 Ari	15 Gem	14 Gem	15 Leo	15 Vir	16 Sco	16 Sag	16 Aqu	15 Pis	14 Ari	15 Gem	15 Can
16 Tau	17 Can	17 Can	18 Vir	18 Lib	18 Sag	18 Cap	18 Pis	17 Ari	16 Tau	17 Can	17 Leo
18 Gem	20 Leo	19 Leo	20 Lib	20 Sco	20 Cap	20 Aqu	20 Ari	19 Tau	19 Gem	20 Leo	20 Vir
21 Can	22 Vir	22 Vir	22 Sco	22 Sag	22 Aqu	22 Pis	23 Tau	21 Gem	21 Can	22 Vir	22 Lib
24 Leo	25 Lib	24 Lib	25 Sag	24 Cap	24 Pis	24 Ari	25 Gem	24 Can	24 Leo	25 Lib	25 Sco
26 Vir	27 Sco	26 Sco	27 Cap	26 Aqu	27 Ari	26 Tau	27 Can	26 Leo	26 Vir	27 Sco	27 Sag
28 Lib		28 Sag	29 Aqu	28 Pis	29 Tau	29 Gem	30 Leo	29 Vir	28 Lib	29 Sag	29 Cap
31 Sco		30 Cap		30 Ari		31 Can			31 Sco		31 Aqu

1969

JAN.	FEB.	MAR.	APR.	MAY	JUN.	JUL.	AUG.	SEP.	OCT.	NOV.	DEC.
2 Pis	2 Tau	2 Tau	3 Can	3 Leo	1 Vir	1 Lib	2 Sag	3 Cap	3 Pis	1 Ari	1 Gem
4 Ari	5 Gem	4 Gem	5 Leo	5 Vir	4 Lib	4 Sco	5 Cap	3 Aqu	5 Ari	3 Tau	5 Can
6 Tau	7 Can	6 Can	8 Vir	8 Lib	6 Sco	6 Sag	7 Aqu	5 Pis	7 Tau	5 Gem	7 Leo
9 Gem	10 Leo	9 Leo	10 Lib	10 Sco	9 Sag	8 Cap	9 Pis	7 Ari	9 Gem	7 Can	9 Vir
11 Can	12 Vir	12 Vir	13 Sco	12 Sag	11 Cap	10 Aqu	11 Ari	9 Tau	11 Can	10 Leo	12 Lib
13 Leo	15 Lib	14 Lib	15 Sag	14 Cap	13 Aqu	12 Pis	13 Tau	11 Gem	13 Leo	12 Vir	15 Sco
16 Vir	17 Sco	16 Sco	17 Cap	17 Aqu	15 Pis	14 Ari	15 Gem	14 Can	16 Vir	15 Lib	17 Sag
18 Lib	19 Sag	19 Sag	19 Aqu	19 Pis	17 Ari	16 Tau	17 Can	16 Leo	18 Lib	17 Sco	19 Cap
21 Sco	22 Cap	21 Cap	21 Pis	21 Ari	19 Tau	19 Gem	20 Leo	19 Vir	21 Sco	19 Sag	21 Aqu
23 Sag	24 Aqu	23 Aqu	24 Ari	23 Tau	21 Gem	21 Can	22 Vir	21 Lib	23 Sag	22 Cap	23 Pis
25 Cap	26 Pis	25 Pis	26 Tau	25 Gem	24 Can	24 Leo	25 Lib	24 Sco	25 Cap	24 Aqu	25 Ari
27 Aqu	28 Ari	27 Ari	28 Gem	27 Can	26 Leo	26 Vir	27 Sco	26 Sag	28 Aqu	26 Pis	28 Tau
29 Pis		29 Tau	30 Can	30 Leo	29 Vir	29 Lib	30 Sag	28 Cap	30 Pis	28 Ari	30 Gem
31 Ari		31 Gem				31 Sco		30 Aqu		30 Tau	

Astro-Tips

THE NATURAL ZODIAC

HOUSE	SEASON	SIGN	HOURS	RULER	RULES
First	Spring	Aries	4–6 a.m.	Mars	Head
Second	Spring	Taurus	2–4 a.m.	Venus	Neck
Third	Spring	Gemini	12–2 a.m.	Mercury	Arms
Fourth	Summer	Cancer	10–12 mid.	Moon	Breast
Fifth	Summer	Leo	8–10 p.m.	Sun	Heart
Sixth	Summer	Virgo	6–8 p.m.	Mercury	Bowels
Seventh	Autumn	Libra	4–6 p.m.	Venus	Kidneys
Eighth	Autumn	Scorpio	2–4 p.m.	Mars	Secrets
Ninth	Autumn	Sagittarius	12–2 p.m.	Jupiter	Thighs
Tenth	Winter	Capricorn	10–12 noon	Saturn	Knees
Eleventh	Winter	Aquarius	8–10 a.m.	Uranus	Calves
Twelfth	Winter	Pisces	6–8 a.m.	Neptune	Feet

MORE ABOUT THE SIGNS

SIGN	GENDER	KEY WORDS	ATTRIBUTE	EXPRESSION
Aries	Masculine	I am	Ardor	Aspiration
Taurus	Feminine	I have	Stamina	Integration
Gemini	Masculine	I think	Diversity	Reason
Cancer	Feminine	I feel	Domesticity	Expansion
Leo	Masculine	I will	Courage	Assurance
Virgo	Feminine	I analyze	Purity	Assimilation
Libra	Masculine	I balance	Justice	Equivalence
Scorpio	Feminine	I desire	Desire	Creativity
Sagittarius	Masculine	I see	Reason	Illumination
Capricorn	Feminine	I use	Prudence	Organization
Aquarius	Masculine	I know	Fellowship	Originality
Pisces	Feminine	I believe	Sympathy	Sacrifice

USING FORECASTS

If you read the monthly astrological publications which "forecast" for your Sign, you may find the information given of more benefit to your everyday affairs if you study your ASCENDANT Sign, rather than your Sun Sign exclusively.

Most of these "forecasts" are based upon a Solar Chart which places, in turn, each of the 12 Signs of the Zodiac as the ascendant, and speaks of the activities in the various Houses only in relation to this Solar Chart.

ASTRO-TIPS continued

Unless your Ascendant and Sun Sign are the same, then the various activities mentioned will not necessarily apply to your individual chart.

Remember also that these predictions are of a very broad and general nature, but often do apply very accurately to certain individuals.

MORE ABOUT THE HOUSES

1st House	Rules the personality, the individual disposition and mannerisms, self-interest, and the worldly outlook in general.
2nd House	Rules financial affairs, monetary capabilities — both gains and losses according to influences and aspects.
3rd House	Brothers and sisters, short journeys, creative writing, mental aptitudes and abilities. Can relate to other close family ties.
4th House	The mother (sometimes father), the home and early environment, security, especially late in life. Relates to real estate, property.
5th House	Native's children, nieces and nephews, love affairs, entertainment, pleasures, recreation, show business, hobbies and diversions.
6th House	General health, dealings with employees, servants, and all those who wait upon the native, food, hygiene, clothing, and pets.
7th House	All partnerships — love, marriage, business, recreation. Can denote open enemies, and the public in general.
8th House	Legacies, inheritances, financial affairs of the partner, changes, endings, new beginnings, and different planes of thought.
9th House	Long trips, travel abroad, dreams, vision, expansion, psychic experiences, higher education, intuition, the spiritual.
10th House	The profession, occupation, work, honors, successes, fame, public standing and public relations, the father (or mother).
11th House	Friends, associates, and associations, the financial affairs of the employer, and thought and wishes for the future.
12th House	Unseen or unexpected difficulties, problems of a private nature, secrets, suffering, self-undoing, secret enemies, institutions, the occult.

A TREASURY OF BOOKS

SEPHARIAL'S NEW DICTIONARY OF ASTROLOGY
The Standard Work. Explains all terms
Illustrated; 5¾" x 8¾"; 164 pages; cloth: $4.50

CHEIRO'S WHEN WERE YOU BORN
How your birthdate affects your future
Illustrated; 4¼" x 7⅛"; 128 pages; paper: 95¢; cloth: $3.50

ASTROLOGY
by Ronald C. Davison
Illustrated; 4¼" x 7⅛"; 176 pages; paper: 95¢ cloth: $3.50

CHEIRO'S LANGUAGE OF THE HAND
The Classic of Palmistry
Illustrated; 4⅛" x 7"; 240 pages; paper: 95¢ cloth: $3.50

CHEIRO'S BOOK OF NUMBERS
A Masterpiece on the Science of Numerology
Illustrated; 4¼" x 7⅛"; 192 pages; paper: 95¢ cloth: $3.50

CHEIRO'S PALMISTRY FOR ALL
A concise handbook for beginners and experts
Illustrated; 4¼" x 7⅛"; 144 pages; paper: 95¢ cloth: $3.50

All books are available at your bookseller or directly from ARCO PUBLISHING COMPANY INC., 219 Park Avenue South, New York, N.Y. 10003. Send price of books plus 25¢ for postage and handling. Sorry, no C.O.D.